Your Gifted Child

How to Recognize and Develop the Special Talents in Your Child from Birth to Age Seven

JOAN FRANKLIN SMUTNY,
KATHLEEN VEENKER,
and STEPHEN VEENKER

Facts On File

New York • Oxford

Your Gifted Child: How to Recognize and Develop the Special Talents in Your Child from Birth to Age Seven

Facts On File®
460 Park Avenue South
New York, New York 10016

Library of Congress Cataloging-in-Publication Data

Smutney, Joan Franklin.
    Your gifted child: how to recognize and develop the special talents in your child from birth to age seven / Joan Franklin Smutny, Kathleen Veenker, and Stephen Veenker.
        p. cm.
    Includes index.
    ISBN 0-8160-1663-1
    1. Gifted children—Identification. 2. Giften children—Education. 3. Education—Parent participation. I. Veenker, Kathleen. II. Veenker, Stephen. III. Title.
HQ773.5.S58 1989   88-27411
371.45′2—dc19

British CIP data available on request
Text Design by Facts On File, Inc.
Jacket Design by Catherine Hyman
Composition by Facts On File, Inc.

Printed in the United States of America

10 9 8 7 6 5 4 3 2 1

Contents

Acknowledgments

This book, truly a labor of love, was made possible by hundreds of caring, sharing parents and professionals, who took the time to give us their insights and perspectives. The remarkable preschool and primary faculty at Creative Children's Academy, most especially Debbie Mc-Grath, and the dedicated faculty and staff of the Center for Gifted, National College of Education, especially Cheryl Siewers and Erin Wiggins, shared their special views and problem-solving techniques. Moreover, the hundreds of parents who call us in the course of any given year have over the years defined the scope and nature of looking for goodness-of-fit for their children and countless solutions to problems that confront us all. School administrators Tom Powers and Michael Horvich and countless dedicated teachers granted us access to their dominions and shared their professional experiences. Marion Wilson, director of the Early Education Programs for the Ferguson-Florissant (Mo.) school district, was most helpful. Hours of labor came from Gwen Gage, and her research and shared experiences with preschool children were most helpful. So many respected writers graciously allowed us to relay their writing. Dorothy Sisk gave us encouragement and contributed her gracious assessment in her foreword. Every one of them contributes a thread to this tapestry.

Finally, there are three unindicted co-conspirators, without whose contributions this book would not exist: Tom Biracree, who demonstrated that you don't have to knock on many doors if you know which one to knock on first; Gerry Helferich, whose wisdom, guidance, patience, and unfailing faith gave us great encouragement; and Rita Haynes Blocksom, a sensitive and supportive reader and editor who has, in the words of the country preacher's prayer, "filled our mouth with worthwhile stuff . . . and nudged us when we've said enough." To each of these goes our lasting and loving gratitude.

Joan Franklin Smutny
Kathleen Veenker
Stephen Veenker

Dedicated to . . .

. . . our children—Cheryl, Matthew, James, Beth, Erin, Kate,
   from whom we learn so much each day
. . . our parents and first teachers
. . . the countless parents we hear from every day,
   who in asking questions are themselves a source
   of insight and inspiration
. . . and the thousands of children,
   who have taken us into their worlds of wonder through the years

Foreword

Most responsible parents want their children to develop strong minds and strong bodies, and they are willing to provide their children with the time and activities that will foster such development. And most parents think their children are special, but they are confused about whether or not their child could be one of the talented ones, one of the gifted.

This book by Joan Franklin Smutny, Stephen Veenker, and Kathleen Veenker offers parents information on child development and tips on how to identify and nurture giftedness. If young children are to become gifted and productive, they are most likely to have come from a family that communicates and shares enthusiastic commitments to family activities. This book offers parents the needed insights and expertise to become advocates for their gifted child both in the family and at home.

The need for this book is tremendous. As previous director of the Office of Gifted and Talented in Washington, DC, and currently as executive director for the World Council for Gifted and Talented, I can testify to the thousands of calls from parents for information and assistance that we have received. Parents need to know that gifted children require special recognition and appreciation. They also need to have answers to their questions that represent enlightened responses. This book does just that. It is factual, practical, and written with a sense of sustained caring that comes from the fact that the authors truly understand the gifted child.

In this book the authors offer parents a more effective approach for dealing with complex issues within the family. Their ideas are based on the notion that the family can foster a supportive and nurturing climate. Parents who will make the commitment to provide the time and reflectively read this book will be more able to develop their children's ability. This book offers the vehicle.

Your Gifted Child will be helpful to teachers and librarians and other community leaders, indeed to all those individuals who seek to offer encouragement to gifted children and their parents. Through their book the authors are endeavoring to help prepare the way for gifted children, and as a result are helping to prepare the way for a better tomorrow for society.

Dorothy Sisk

Introduction

A child was taken to see a testing psychologist because his parents suspected he had taught himself to read. Suspicion confirmed: he was reading, the tester told them, at second-grade level. Not bad for a 29-month-old.

While playing informally with a jigsaw map, a mother handed her 3-year-old one of the pieces and mentioned that it was Kansas. "That's where Dorothy and Toto lived," the girl replied. Had the girl seen a recent broadcast of *The Wizard of Oz*? No, she remembered seeing a video borrowed from the library: "We took it back the day we got *Betsy and Peter*." A full year earlier.

After a friend showed her 2-year-old a song on the black keys of their piano, the child surprised his mother days later by playing it back accurately, transposed to a different key, and using only the white keys.

A 4-year-old stopped to study the way a light rainfall was drying from a patch of smooth but pockmarked concrete. "It looks," she said, "like the skin of a potato."

Terry always understood math. At 2 she could count to 100. At 3 1/2 she was her mother's assistant grocery shopper, and could estimate the total cost of the bill with surprising accuracy.

Which of these children is "gifted"?

Of course, they all are.

To some people, giftedness brings to mind the highly intelligent child who remembers everything he has studied and can cough it up on exam day for perfect test scores. But being a speed-reader with total recall is only one facet of what we call gifted, and only part of all gifted kids are like that.

Consider this excellent comparison, which we found in a reprint attributed to a writer named Yatvin in the Gifted Child Newsletter, between exceptionally bright children and those who are gifted as well:

> *Bright children* keep the system going. They take music lessons, read library books, join clubs, collect things, do their homework, enjoy group activities, play Scrabble and tennis, follow directions ... get good grades, win and display trophies, and seek the leadership of adults. [They're]

willing to learn whatever their teachers deem important in order to achieve their major goals, to advance and to fulfill their societal responsibilities.

Gifted children, on the other hand, while displaying many of the same characteristics, also lead, dare, innovate, dream and solve problems. They sell lemonade, form clubs, make things out of junk, read comic books and Shakespeare, invent games, take apart their bicycles, enter contests . . . and get erratic grades, make fantasy lands out of their bedrooms, and avoid adult-dominated activities, . . . choosing what they will learn in order to perform worthwhile tasks, solve problems and discover meaning, order, and beauty. Getting ahead, pleasing and meeting the expectations of society are of secondary importance.

Another excellent treatment of the nature of giftedness, published in the *Roeper Review*, November, 1983, is by Dr. Leslie Kaplan, adjunct faculty at the College of William and Mary and author of *Coping with Peer Pressure*:

Gifted students can learn material faster. They can think new information through and grasp its meaning more quickly than do their peers. . . .

Gifted young people learn deeper. They make connections among separate bits of information, develop relationships within the data, and build concepts. They take different ideas and make a coherent whole. Gifted young people manipulate the information they learn. They actively analyze and recombine facts to create new information. . . .

They are resourceful problem solvers and contribute improved solutions. Many investigators find that interests, attitudes, and motivation, not intelligence alone, set the gifted apart from their classmates.

Until recently most schools treated giftedness as a phenomenon that materializes somehow in the late primary grades—around 8 years of age. That's when it is first perceived by school systems because that's when many teachers first look for it.

The sudden manifestation seems to correlate with a stage at which a bright child "psyches out" test taking. They become proficient in giving right answers and find themselves scoring in the high ninetieth percentiles compared to national averages. If their school district has a gifted program for, let's say, the five percent who score highest on the group achievement tests, they find themselves labeled "gifted" and incorporated in a "gifted program."

But suppose they move to a different district, which, like the old neighborhood, has a program, but uses an IQ of 140 as the cutoff for participation. Is the child no longer gifted? Was she in the first place?

Moreover, if giftedness is properly defined above, will a truly gifted child be identified by either group achievement tests *or* the individual IQ tests? Not always. Screening and testing are like fishing with nets; some of the prized specimens slip through. Some common kinds of giftedness just don't show up on intelligence tests—leadership, artistic ability, a feeling for musical theory, heightened sensitivity to others' feelings, and awareness of his own feelings.

This testing/identifying imbalance is only one of a long string of roadblocks, ambiguities, and misadventures the gifted child may encounter along the way to his place in the community. You won't find uniformity or consensus in our schools' handling of gifted students. What to do with gifted children is a subjective, political, emotional issue for a school board. The treatment and accommodation offered to your child may vary from grade to grade, from school to school, and even from day to day.

Many people feel that if a child is gifted, or even perceived to be gifted, he is exceptional in every area, immune from disappointment or frustration, and eternally self-sufficient. Like most stereotypes, these are inaccurate and misleading.

A better assessment of the consequences of giftedness comes from Anne-Marie Roeper, headmistress of the Roeper Lower School, which appeared in the *Gifted Child Quarterly*, No. 3, 1977:

> Giftedness really is an ability to think, to generalize, to see connections and to use alternatives. The abilities just described may not necessarily translate themselves into outstanding academic achievement at a preschool level or even at a later level. . . .
>
> Yet the young child gifted with superior thinking abilities . . . may not be ready to deal emotionally with that which he/she understands intellectually. . . .
>
> The gifted child is not necessarily ahead of others academically. Often people confuse giftedness with precociousness. Other children catch up with the precocious child later.

The best hope a gifted child has is for an informed parent—to pave the way, prepare his expectations, enrich his surroundings, bridge gaps, open doors, leap obstacles, build confidence, and produce change where it is needed.

Parents are, after all, the first and most important teachers a child has, and, in the years before the identification process even begins in school, they are particularly significant.

Are the child's special gifts lying dormant on some kind of cerebral back burner, waiting to be warmed up on the eighth birthday? Of course not. We are learning that the child's giftedness—partly genetic and partly environmental—has been developing all along. Maybe it's been manifesting itself in subtle ways for years. Many studies conclude that parents are quite receptive to the behavioral clues that point to exceptional talent.

But were also learning, as we race toward the twenty-first century, that children are quite complex and marvelous creatures *from the moment of birth*. If a large proportion of mental development occurs before the fifth birthday, as indeed it does, must we not nurture exceptional gifts from the beginning? When you hope to encourage the kind of thinking that makes connections, we feel that stimulation and encouragement work a lot better than flash cards with new words or math facts. Better to nurture the kinds of observation and analyses that become wit and wisdom as the years go by.

In the extreme, pressures to produce children who excel among their peers have given rise to a phenomenon known as "superbaby," a trend so significant that it got a cover story in *Time* magazine. Parents of superbabies want them to be the first to acquire teeth, walk, read, recite the alphabet, play a musical instrument, and be accepted by the "best" college, though not necessarily in that order.

In our opinion, nothing of lasting value is gained by breeding or cloning superbabies. People who know their child only in comparison to when their neighbors' children first walked, or talked, or did three-digit subtraction in their heads, are missing the whole point of being in touch with their own child, helping her become all that she can be, and enjoying what makes her an individual. Pumping her full of skills is not the same as encouraging her to develop her own gifts and abilities.

Will a book make your child gifted? No. Nor will a class, or a teacher, or a set of books, or a computer. If potential giftedness is already present, there are things that books, and teachers, and parents can do to encourage its development. There are stories of individuals with great gifts that develop under adversity. These are worth retelling precisely because they represent exceptions to the general rule. We don't tell stories about the children of exceptional promise who are never heard from again after being shunted off into the shadows of Special Ed classes or Behavioral Disorder sections because of a faulty diagnosis somewhere along the way.

We have seen enrichment and encouragement help giftedness develop—as children come to grips with their abilities and learn to manage their potentials instead of leaving them undeveloped.

Our observations come from raising our own and others' children, counseling with hundreds of parents, and observing literally thousands of identified gifted children in the Chicago area who have enrolled in various afterschool and weekend enrichment programs and/or a full-time private school for gifted children.

Working with parents of gifted children has reminded us again and again that there are no reliable and generally available books offering guidance for parents of young gifted children. In the pages ahead we help identify some of the common signs of giftedness and help parents gauge their own children's characteristics.

We deal with some of the things you can be doing in the early years from infancy through the preschool years until school programs and other enhancements keep the coals glowing. We take more of a holistic approach to the kinds of environments that encourage giftedness, more than tab-A-in-slot-B directions. Giftedness doesn't come from a recipe, a blueprint, a road map, or a rule book. On the other hand, the activities we recommend will stimulate all children, so don't throw this book away if someone "accuses" your child of being normal.

We also talk about schools—choosing the right preschool, kindergarten, and primary programs, matching programs with your child's strengths, what to do until your school district serves its gifted population (and what to do if they don't even try). We discuss the kinds of supplemental programs that are available and how to help create them if they aren't. Having gifted kids doesn't mean your problems are over; it means you may face a different set of problems. We talk about some of the headaches and some of the solutions as well.

Good advice and resources are at hand in the form of books, projects, and pamphlets, and more are coming every day. They're not in every corner store, but we share what we've found to be available and try to make them easier for you to find than they were for us.

A word about advice, especially for new parents. Many of the best resources we've found deal not with gifted children but with children as whole people. (After all, how effective can a gifted person be if no one wants to be around him?) Welcome to the information age: you can now find a book that will tell you almost everything about practically anything. Books on parenting abound, but no single book can provide the perspective you may need. Only by synthesizing guidance from several sources can you, in partnership with your child, become what Bruno Bettelheim calls the Good Enough Parent. You can provide and enrich, enable and encourage those special aspects that may one day lead to something quite magical.

The experts we turn to most often for authoritative advice on child development often differ on specific points. We've always been able to balance and contrast and take what works for us and our children. But when we began to take comparative notes, we were delighted to find them agreeing on one enormously important point. And here it is, virtually the same in the writings of Burton White, Joan Beck, Bruno Bettelheim, T. Berry Brazelton, and Dr. Spock (the pediatrician, not the Vulcan):

One: No single book has all the answers, including this one; and

Two: When what you read seems all wrong for your particular situation, trust your instinct over the experts' opinions, because *nobody knows your child better than you do.*

Great Expectations: Laying a Foundation in Infancy

Our task would be easier if we knew right away whether a newborn was going to be gifted a few years later. We can buy birth announcements with spaces for all the so-called vital statistics: 8 pounds, 4 ounces; 6:55 A.M.; 21½ inches. We've never found one with a blank for IQ.

Nor are we likely to. It might be valuable to have a good, reliable index of a child's potential soon after he is born, but there simply isn't one. Some pediatricians use a scale devised by Dr. Virginia Apgar to record an impression of a newborn's general vitality—skin color, muscle tone, alertness, and responsiveness. Such a score may be a helpful diagnostic at the moment of birth, but we're grateful that it doesn't seem to have caught on as a status symbol ("My baby was a 9 Apgar, yours was an 8, but hers was a 6").

Intelligence, of course, can't yet be measured with unfailing accuracy. We can, and do, get more finite in the middle- and upper-school grades with battery after battery of tests—intelligence tests, achievement tests, and a host of others we discuss in another chapter. You can give intelligence tests to very young children, and you can even use the equivalent of an IQ score to describe their comparative mental development. But you can't always use a number on an infant's test to predict her IQ at age 10. Few studies have found a reliable correlation. Some

1

studies show 4-year-old children's test data to be consistent with results at age 7. Intelligence tests depend too heavily on verbal skills to yield reliable predictive results in infants

Does this mean nobody knows who's gifted till schools start fishing for them?

No. Almost every educator of gifted children subscribes to the conventional wisdom that parents are reliable observers and identifiers of giftedness. One University of Michigan study, for example, reported in *Psychology in the Schools*, Vol. 8, pp. 140-142, followed up a group of children who took intelligence tests at early ages. When they were older, nineteen of these children had IQs of 135 or higher. While none of them had been identified as exceptional in the early tests, parents of sixteen had correctly identified them as potentially gifted, based on their observations at home.

A study in 1983 entitled "Gifted Infants" conducted by SENG (Supporting 'Emotional Needs of Gifted [Wright State University, Dayton, Ohio]) surveyed parents of 1,000 formally identified (that is, "tested") gifted children. Among other things, the survey asked parents at what age they "first suspected" their children were gifted. Eighty-three percent said it was before kindergarten. Twenty-two percent said they guessed correctly before their children's first birthday.

Our own interviews of parents of gifted children substantiate that many, though by no means all, somehow intuited what was in store for them when their children were still quite young. One father, who had participated in religious ceremonies for newborns for years, said he was amazed when his own child was born: he had never seen such a calm, focused gaze in any other child.

A teacher of gifted children tells us that she has several highly reliable early indicators, among them an alertness and curiosity that demand stimulation; the ability to function with less sleep than other children; acute and mature perceptions that seem to soak up information like a sponge and understand the world and how it works; and a mixture of exploration and sense of humor.

FELICIA AND DAVID: EXAMPLES OF TWO GIFTED CHILDREN

Since there are no tests we can give an infant that accurately predict giftedness, several studies have taken formally identified older gifted

children and looked carefully at the kind of behavior and surroundings they came from. One of the most striking is a study by Janet Brown done in two parts and reported in the *Merrill-Palmer Quarterly* No. 10 (1964) and 16 (1970) and summarized by Michael Lewis and Linda Michaelson of Rutgers Medical School in *The Psychology of Gifted Children*, 1986. Brown made exhaustive notes on the behavior of a group of newborns, tracked the children through the middle grades, determined that one girl was of vastly superior talents, and compared her behavior to that of the others in infancy.

The girl's name is Felicia. As an 8-year-old she showed Brown "not only superior intelligence but also unusual artistic ability." When studied as a newborn, Felicia even stood out from her nursery companions. She seemed older, more responsive to external stimuli, ready to process sensory perceptions, and somehow more in control of her surroundings. That is, when crying she would stop at the introduction of a visual stimulus, and when fussy she could be calmed by the sound of a human voice alone—no holding or hugging or swaddling were required. She resisted being moved and didn't particularly like to be cuddled.

Felicia was unusually responsive to her environment. She was the only neonate who mimicked facial expressions; the only one whose eyes scanned a stationary visual stimulus, and she responded to visual and auditory stimuli in a way not normally seen in infants under 2 or 3 weeks of age. Hospital personnel soon noticed "her expressive face and wide-eyed gaze," dubbing her "the personality kid."

Whether or not her independence can be called a manifestation of what would later become her artistic creativity, or her visual attentiveness a sign of high intellect, Felicia clearly stood out from the crowd from the moment of birth. People who worked in the hospital nursery could identify and describe a number of quite specific qualities that separated her from the mainstream.

Some of the characteristics of Felicia bring to mind the case of David, a gifted youngster described by one of our interviewees. Even before he was born, David's mother wondered if the cutesy-cuddly syndrome was indigenous to newborns or culturally derived. Did all babies coo like the ones in the diaper commercials? The parents resolved to listen faithfully for his cues instead of anticipating his needs. "If babies get 'babied' excessively," they reasoned, "why would they bother to think, act or do anything?"

When David was still very young, his mother would put him on the floor of their living room, then draw back a bit to watch him. He soon began

> scuttling about on his stomach like a fish on water, poking into everything. He couldn't have been more than three months. I would find him running his finger over objects, turning them around in his tiny hands and examining them with tremendous concentration. His attention span at the age of five months on only a few simple objects, at times spanned over an hour or two. He never got tired of handling new objects, moving them around and letting out shrieks of delight every once in a while as he squirmed over to another part of the room.

David was a child who flourished with a minimum of gooing and cooing. His parents correctly intuited what worked for him, and were attentive and empathic without doing what they called pampering. "I have never seen such a young child express such individuality, peace of mind, and fearlessness," reported a qualified observer, "a genuinely peaceful child . . . empowered by his parents . . . so much the adventurous explorer."

An observant parent is indispensable. If David had needed more cuddling his mother and father would have recognized it. The child who isn't comfortable being held will let you know with muscle tone and body language. One of the infant's first problem-solving behaviors is to conform to a holding parent. They can turn to Jell-O and become impossible to hold when they want to, and awfully hard to put down when they want to be held.

In fact, long before the child can tell you verbally what's going on, he has a whole vocabulary of signs and symbols that he uses at will to make his wishes known. Infants routinely use their nonverbal vocabulary of rich and expressive nuances. Sensitive parents perceive it, understand, and respond, still at the nonverbal level.

A recent book by Evelyn Thoman called *Born Dancing* describes this kind of communication, which when spoken fluently by both parent and child leads to the essential "goodness-of-fit." The title metaphor refers to the kind of stylized interchange of eye contact, body motions, and vocalization that babies and mothers instinctively perform. It is one step away from a formalized dance, the intricate pas de deux in which each partner reacts constantly with the other. The sensitive partner is always aware of subtle signals and changes; so it is with the infant and parent who are attuned.

The better the fit, the closer the dance, the keener the perception, the better the chance that an infant's first signs of giftedness will be recognized. Once identified, potential giftedness can be encouraged.

EARLY SIGNS OF GIFTEDNESS

The earliest studies of gifted children, more than half a century ago, first gave us the reassurance that early development of skills is in fact a positive indicator. If your child walks, talks, understands, feeds himself, or otherwise demonstrates motor skills *earlier* than his siblings or age-mates, this child *may* be potentially gifted.

Let's emphasize two basic givens before we go further. One: Any or all of these early signs may be positive indicators, but cannot accurately predict or guarantee the presence of giftedness later on. Two: The absence of any or all of these indicators doesn't mean a child is not gifted. If it sounds as if we're hedging our bets, remember that we have no infallibly accurate way to measure giftedness; we can only describe its manifestations.

Beyond motor skills, a second area to monitor involves quantities: the child knows more words, has a longer attention span, speaks longer and more complex sentences, and demonstrates faster learning and greater appetite for books and pictures. Gifted children, their parents tell us later, would sit patiently far longer than others—through longer books, more books, more repetitions of the same book than others.

A third area is based on comparisons. The gifted child tends to find more ways to use toys and tools; decipher codes, patterns, and puzzles; initiate new play activities; imagine more creative situations; and demonstrate a deeper understanding of questions and answers from older people.

Other early signs described by Rita Haynes Blocksom, a consultant to school systems, are: good recall; the use of trial and error in solving problems; entertaining himself for large blocks of time; and finding incongruities humorous.

Remember that, unlike frozen vegetables arriving from the factory with Universal Product Code stripes printed on the package, babies don't arrive with IQ scores. Nobody can tell you that your infant, now 3 months old, will or won't be more or less gifted than another. We have spoken to parents of hundreds of children identified as gifted, and many have told us of hunches they had in the delivery room. We can't prove their hunches were wrong, but we haven't interviewed parents of non-gifted kids to ask them when they first thought their kids *weren't* gifted.

WHAT *DO* WE KNOW?

Although many attempts have been made to predict giftedness with clinical accuracy before a child's second birthday, we know of no data supporting an ability to predict giftedness. There are, however, some fascinating studies that shed light on behavior as an index. Visual attentiveness appears to be the most reliable touchstone. At New York University and Albert Einstein College of Medicine, independent research by Marc Bornstein and by Susan Rose and reported in *Science* (May 15, 1987) demonstrated a strong correlation between visual attentiveness in the first six months of life and high IQ scores at age 4 to 6 years. High IQ scores *and* the visual attention indicator were present in between twenty-four and thirty-six percent of the subjects—surely not an empirical link, but arguably one of the closest correlatives recorded to date.

For Rose and Bornstein the correlation between the initial eye movement and the process that seeks new stimuli when the familiar one is recognized may well be our first link to the emergence of mental processes. "Clearly, we think we're into information processing," Bornstein told *Science*, "into capturing how the organism deals with details. Dealing with novelty is what life is all about."

Further evidence of a link between early visual attentiveness and later identification of giftedness is detailed by Rutgers Medical School's Child Development Division chief, Professor Michael Lewis, and Assistant Professor Linda Michaelson, in a chapter of *The Psychology of Gifted Children*. They cite work reported in 1981 by J. F. Fagan of Case Western Reserve University and S. K. McGrath which "have shown that early measures of attention are actually better predictors of subsequent cognitive ability than standard IQ tests." One indicator was the rapidity with which the newborns would actively redirect their attention to a new visual stimulus—in other words, get bored with one picture and shift their gaze to a new one. Part of this behavior is recognizing a picture seen previously and retained in memory.

But which is the horse and which is the cart? Does the visual atten-tiveness merely serve as the first visible indicator of other innate factors that follow inevitably? Or is giftedness merely a larger aspect of the kind of information processing first manifested as visual attentiveness?

"The reality," Lewis and Michaelson conclude, "may be that during infancy there is only a potential for giftedness that requires some 'optimal' environment for development. In contrast to a handicapping condition giftedness may not exist early in life, but emerge only as the product of interaction between infants' genetic endowments and the environments in which they are raised."

Many experts believe that giftedness evolves under optimum condi-tions, dependent on genetic capacity, the environment, and the *quality of nurturance*, or the "goodness-of-fit" we discussed earlier. Self-concept, emotional adjustment, encouragement by family, teachers, and peers, and, always, the stimulation of the child's surroundings are parts of this "goodness-of-fit" on the journey to maturity

LAYING A FOUNDATION IN INFANCY

Before conception the mother's health, and even the father's physical condition, can affect the future brain of their child, as can the emotional environment of the developing fetus.

Jane Healy, Ph.D., of Cleveland State University in *Your Child's Grow-ing Mind*, states that "the growing brain is highly susceptible to struc-tural, chemical, and hormonal influences. For example, some researchers believe that specific academic abilities, such as reading or math, may be affected by hormones secreted during pregnancy."

Fear, anger, stress, and anxiety trigger chemical responses in the mother's body, Healy continues. Since her bloodstream is the source of the baby's nutrients, it doesn't take a lot of imagination to envision the fetal brain being affected to some degree. In *The Secret Life of the Unborn Child*, T. Verny cites evidence that excessive emotional stress during pregnancy may produce hyperactive and irritable infants. While this in itself may not affect intellectual potential, it may make the newborn infant more difficult to deal with and, by affecting the parent-child relationship, hinder early development. Understanding the causes may help the parent to overcome these effects.

Others feel that activities such as playing music or reading to the child while he is in the womb may enhance development. It's likely that the unborn child perceives sounds. Some mothers have noticed their third-trimester babies seem to startle at loud noises.

In the third edition of *Growing Up Gifted* Barbara Clark cites T. Verny's compilation of several research projects that indicates the fetus reacts to sounds and even melodies in the fourth or fifth month. "Vivaldi and Mozart cause the child to relax," Clark quotes, while "Beethoven and Brahms stimulate movement." It has been further reported that the fetus hears clearly from the sixth month in *utero* and can be seen to move in rhythm to the mother's speech.

Dr. Anthony DeCasper of the University of North Carolina has concluded that 3-day-old newborns show a preference for the sound of their mother's voice over a stranger's voice, and prefer the same story read to them daily in the last 6 weeks before birth to an unfamiliar story.

In any event, the principal benefit of such activities as playing music to a pregnant woman in such a way that it can be heard by the unborn infant may be in providing a calm time for the mother-to-be that may carry over after birth into a shared time of relaxation for mother and child.

The birth experience itself is a major factor in the environment of the developing child. A medication-free, noninterventionist birth contributes to an alert newborn and a positive bonding experience between parents and child.

Infants enjoy a state of awareness, about ten percent of any given waking hour, when they will demonstrate a preference for faces and turn their heads to follow spoken voices. Klaus and Kennell, in *Parent-Infant Bonding*, point out that this quiet-alert state accounts for about forty-five minutes of the first hour after delivery. At this point the baby sees, reacts to sounds, and moves his head in the direction of voices. Then the weary traveler drifts into several hours of deep sleep. This "quiet-alert" stage is also present for about ten percent of the first weeks, so don't worry if you missed it at birth.

We have long known that the newborn's eyes focus best at about 10 to 12 inches. Many believe that's the perfect range to allow eye contact with the nursing mother.

Breast-feeding can also contribute to a best start. Not only does it enhance the bonding of mother and child but also the child's overall health. Dr. Burton White, founder and director of the Center for Parent Education in Newton, Ma., and author of *The First Three Years of Life*, stresses the value of breast-feeding in reducing the rate of recurrent otitis media, or middle ear infection, associated with temporary hearing loss that may seriously impede a child's learning ability.

All these factors can contribute to the optimizing of a child's potential. A healthy pregnancy helps ensure a healthy brain. A good birth experience, breast-feeding, and time for bonding help pave the way for responsiveness between parents and child. A belief that any one influence is critical, however, denies the immense complexity of the human brain. Healy notes that the newborn brain "is wonderfully malleable to experience," and "much can be done after birth to ameliorate earlier problems." Pediatrician and best-selling author Dr. T. Berry Brazelton emphasizes in *On Becoming a Family* that the essence of good parenting lies not in specific things one does for one's baby but in establishing an intensely rewarding feedback between parents and child. The baby's own inborn personality will also play a part in this exchange. To fully nurture giftedness, the parents must first recognize the marvelous complexity of their newborn child. The parents' belief in the high potential of their child and treatment of that child as a developing person of worth can help develop a strong sense of self and initiative in the child.

In *Optimizing Learning*, Barbara Clark of California State University notes:

> From the moment of birth each human infant has over 100 billion neural cells in the brain ready for use, and is capable of creating trillions of connections for learning, memory storage and retrieval, problem solving, rational and abstract thinking, sophisticated motoric involvement, emotional expression, and intuitive and creative production . . . in short, the use of intelligence. It is believed that most humans use only a small percentage of this vast potential, and of this potential far more is lost than is actualized in a lifetime.

We believe parents can make the difference in the actualization of this vast potential.

Building the Infant's Self-Image

As recently as the early 1960s the mind of the newborn was thought to be relatively primitive. Today we know it to be a complex and wondrous organ.

What caused the change in views? Did babies get smarter in one generation? Or did researchers become more insightful?

The answer is probably both. The more researchers can tell us about the workings and capabilities of the brains of our babies, the more we are able to do as parents.

One revolutionary step toward understanding newborns' behavior actually took place independently on two different continents. In Boston, child psychiatrist Dr. Peter Wolf filmed details of behavior of newborns in their homes. Independently, Dr. Heinz Prechtl in Groningen, Holland, observed and recorded breathing, brain wave, and heartbeat data in Dutch newborns.

Analyzing the masses of quantitative data they gathered, Wolf and Prechtl found that what seem to be random activities are in fact classifiable into six patterns of states of consciousness among newborn babies:

1. Quiet-Alert: eyes open, bright, shiny; motor activity suppressed. In this stage babies' eyes can follow a moving object and choose between two shapes; some babies appear to imitate exaggerated facial expressions. Seen as much as forty-five minutes of the first hour after a normal, uncomplicated delivery and ten percent of all waking hours in the first days of life.
2. Active-Alert: eyes and limbs move frequently and baby makes small sounds. Occurs before eating and when baby would be called "fussy." Every minute or two the baby moves arms, legs, body or face; similar bursts of movement have been detected in the uterus.
3. Crying: face contorted and red; arms and legs move; eyes may be open or tightly shut.
4. Drowsiness: between sleep and wakefulness. Eyes dull, glazed, usually not focusing; lids droopy. Baby may continue to move at random.
    Day or night, the newborn sleeps about ninety percent of the time. Two distinct levels of sleep were identified, and babies commonly alternate between the two at roughly thirty-minute intervals.
5. Active sleep: lids closed but sometimes flutter; eyes may move under the lids in REM (rapid eye movements) sleep. Occasional movement; irregular breathing slightly faster than under quiet sleep. Baby sometimes makes faces or chewing or sucking motions.
6. Quiet sleep: deep slumber, few reactions to surroundings. Time to trim baby's nails and vacuum under her crib. Almost nothing will disturb her.

From the close scrutiny newborns have received in the last twenty or thirty years, we are able to gather some very strong evidence for what we can do at home to prepare our little ones for what's ahead.

Ashley Montague, the British anthropologist and prolific author, urges us in *Touching* to consider human gestation as an 18-month process, the first half occurring in the womb. Birth is an important milestone and a connective link to the second 9 months, but merely the midpoint in gestation. Among the primates, only humans put the newborn in a safe place and walk away for long periods of time. Curiously, among humans, only the ones we call highly civilized invent elaborate baby-storage units for the convenience of the parents. Less "advanced" human societies keep their babies with the mother or another human constantly for the first months of life. (How curious it is that these same "backward" tribes know no thumb-sucking!)

Research indicates that newborns are quite sensitive and responsive to the environment. Some believe environmental stimulation leads to actual cellular changes in the brain. But Jane Healey emphasizes in *Your Child's Growing Mind*: "Active interest and mental effort *by the child* is the key."

In *The Amazing Newborn*, Phyllis and Marshall Klaus explain that the nerves that connect vision and hearing centers have developed by birth. And by the time infants are 2 weeks old they link their mother's voice and the sight of her face. Substitute a mask or the sound of another woman's voice, and they nurse less, cry more, and sleep less.

Place food on their tongues, and you will find infants can discern sour, salty, bitter, and sweet. They will show you they prefer sweet.

By the sixth day the newborn can recognize the smell of her mother.

Infants also have well-developed visual interest. Given the choice, they prefer to look at more complex patterns (stripes over solids, wavy lines over straight, small patterns on wallpaper; variety; motion; and facts).

These unusual talents of the newborn may appear at different stages, disappear for a while, and reappear later. Some of this developmental process depends on need, use, underuse, overuse, passivity, and activity. When infants are pushed too much on the one hand, or deprived of various sensory stimuli on the other, their development may be affected. No one knows which skills need to be enhanced or which ones should be left alone.

It is known, however, that infants take delight and interest in a variety of experience.

Providing Warmth and Security

We as parents can become facilitators—we can design the baby's environment to enrich and stimulate him. We can help set the stage for learning and growth by feeling positive about the child, allowing him to feel secure and in control. "Learning seems to occur best," concludes Healy in *Your Child's Growing Mind*, "when positive emotions facilitate chemical secretion in the brain that help messages cross synapses."

The importance of such an atmosphere is clear in the context of Montague's "exterogestation," the second 9 months, in what he calls "the womb with a view." To help meet the child's needs we respond to his cries, which are his first problem-solving link to the rest of the world. He needs our positive reinforcement; he needs to know he is not isolated and can depend on us for nurturance.

The reflexive rocking we instinctively fall into to soothe the baby is no accident; it replicates the motion she knew in the womb. "Rocking reassures the baby," Montague reminds us in *Touching*,

for in its mother's womb it was naturally rocked by the normal motions of her body. To be comfortable means to be comforted, and for the infant this comfort is largely derived from the signals it receives from its skin. The greatest of all comforts is to be cradled in the mother's arms or lap or supported on her back.

Montague goes on to say that "the mother mutually adapted to her child will respond in rhythm to her child's needs. Her flexibility will reflect itself in the child's perceptual development."

In the introduction to his newly revised work, *Infants and Mothers*, T. Berry Brazelton reports,

When I studied the Mayan Indians in Southern Mexico for their early childrearing patterns, I longed for the revival in our society of at least two customs that we as a culture have given up. I longed for mothers to allow themselves more continual physical closeness with their infants, and for the cushioning of the extended family for all young parents.

Our primary goal in the first 7 months of life should be to develop the sense of trust the infant needs to thrive. "The goal of giving the infant a *feeling of being loved and cared for* is, in my judgment, the single most important goal in getting a child off to a good start in life," writes Burton White in *The First Three Years of Life*. "I cannot over-emphasize its importance."

Studying mother-child relationships, University of Michigan researchers under Sheryl Olson's direction followed the growth of youngsters from six months to six years. The 6-year-olds who exhibited good self-control had secure attachments to their mothers before they were 13 months old. At age 2 they had better and more frequent verbal interactions and were disciplined firmly but not harshly. Good self-control enabled the 6-year-olds to "sit still, concentrate, and settle their own disputes peacefully."

This essential comfort should not be confused with "spoiling" a child. In *Psychology Today* (Sept. 1986), White and his colleague Dr. Michael Meyerhoff have written,

> In homes where children were both bright and a pleasure to live with, the parents were not afraid to set realistic but firm boundaries on behavior before the children's first birthday. During the first months of life, these parents lavished love and attention on their children and responded almost unconditionally to every demand. However, starting at about 8 months, and especially during the normal period of "negativism" between 15 and 24 months of age, when many children's demands were simply tests of what they could get away with, these parents reacted by letting the children know in no uncertain terms that other people had rights, too.

Confidence is essential. Infants are affected by the parents' confidence in themselves, which helps establish feelings of security in the infant. "The security of the parents about *being* a parent," writes Dr. Bruno Bettelheim in *The Good Enough Parent*,

> will eventually become the source of the child's feeling secure about himself.
>
> The child's mastery of each new stage of psychological and social development requires understanding and sensitive help from his parents,

so that his later personality will not bear the scars of psychological wounds. The parent must not give in to his desire to try to create the child he would *like* to have, but rather help the child to develop—in his own time—to the fullest, into what he wishes to be and can be, in line with his natural endowment and as the consequence of his unique life history.

Stimulation for the Infant

To encourage the development of sensory perception, smile at and talk to your baby, with lots of eye contact. Respond to his cries, imitate his sounds and expressions. Remember that a good sign of high aptitude is responsiveness and alertness at a comparatively early age.

For visual stimulation, make or buy a mobile designed to be seen from below, preferably with interchangeable designs. Vary it from time to time to keep it interesting. Place posters and graphics 8 to 12 inches from the child's eyes, and to the right (allowing for the typical tonic neck Reflex, which pulls the baby into what is called the "fencer's pose"). Leave a safe, stainless steel unbreakable mirror where it can be seen easily. One mother weaves pieces of bright gift-wrapping paper through the crib slats for an easily changed mural. Place a prism in the window where it will catch sunlight and display a rainbow on the walls. Use patterned sheets and crib bumpers. While big, bold patterns are interesting, smaller patterns actually hold a child's interest longer.

For auditory stimulation, music boxes and record players and tape players work well. Use music of all kinds, children's records by entertainers such as Ella Jenkins and story records from the library to supplement conversation and reading aloud.

Infant seats are lifesavers, allowing you to move about the house and get on with chores without abandoning the baby. At about 3 months, supplement the seat with an arch device from which you can hang crib toys. One, called Toybars, is made by Century Products; other companies have similar offerings. When your baby's neck muscles are stronger, bring in a baby swing, which can calm a troubled child and/or parent. It could save your day, but don't overuse it.

A crib gym with manipulatives—brightly colored objects to encourage reaching and grasping—is useful from 6 weeks to 6 months. A well-designed model has toys suspended with something more rigid than string in order to encourage the child's first grasping efforts. Discontinue its use when the child sits up.

Talk to your baby; touch and stroke her; name body parts as you dress and bathe her. Encourage her to touch various textures as you shop, walk, wait in line, pass a tree, or anything you encounter along your way. Play simple games such as peekaboo and pat-a-cake.

As Klaus and Kennell claim in *Parent-Infant Bonding*, newborns can recognize stories they've heard before birth. Many parents read to their babies from day one. It can't hurt. Your newborn won't understand individual words but the patterns are soothing, not unlike the "comfortable words" of traditional worship. The baby will notice the rhythm patterns of your speech. You can recite nursery rhymes until Little Boy Blue's cows come home.

Beginner books abound. Dick Bruna's *B is for Bear* is one example; you'll be labeling common objects shown on the books' pages. Bruna's deceptively spare style tells stories with bold strokes and primary colors.

Find Dorothy Butler's *Babies Need Books* for a good discussion of the benefits of reading to young infants and suggestions for appropriate material at each age level. Both the original book and its second edition appear to be out of print; if your library can locate a copy, it's well worth the effort.

Of course, keep it simple. Don't force. Too much of a good thing can become tedious. Take cues from your children; give as much as they want, but quit before they've had enough.

When your baby becomes mobile, be absolutely sure your house is childproof. Keep the floors cleared of choking obstacles; put safety plugs in electrical outlets; remember that many plants are toxic. Then give her the run of the place. Fences and gates and pens are for her safety at times when you cannot supervise, not just for your convenience. For best development of the senses and thought processes, let your child have full rein.

Room to move around and explore is vital to his full development. Curiosity is the key to growth.

Toys proliferate, and some of them are quite imaginative. Still, any home is a rich source of stimulation. Remember the old story of the child who receives an expensive educational toy and spends the next two days playing with the box. Nesting measuring cups and spoons from the kitchen drawer are wonderful toys, good for hours of play. But the best toy of all is a responsive and available parent.

2

Toddlerhood
(Eight to Thirty-Six Months)

Your toddler may be gifted if he:

Can sit through hearing a long book and then ask you to read it again

Walks or talks early, or shows early interest in the alphabet

Shows interest in and understands number and time concepts

Can easily do puzzles intended for older children

Compensates for handicaps and learns and functions in spite of them

Shows strong sensitivity and response to music

Remembers complex happenings and describes them long afterword in clear detail

Has an advanced sense of humor or recognizes incongruities as humorous

Retells stories or narrates events clearly and makes up a plausible ending to a story if you stop before the payoff

Picks up songs and poems quickly and repeats them accurately after few hearings

Is impatient with her limitations when her mind can order tasks her body can't yet perform

Knows how things should fit in the scheme of things and is slow to bend when something doesn't conform; is intolerant of something she perceives to be unfair

Consistently organizes, sorts, arranges, classifies, groups things, and then gives them all names

Understands cause and effect, makes inferences, responds to directions, and performs multiple-part tasks earlier than others

Far more may be going on inside your toddler's mind than we might perceive at first glance. All children develop rapidly between 8 and 36 months of age. Talents and abilities are developing; personalities are emerging; individual skills and strengths are becoming more noticeable.

It's the same for the gifted child, except more so, or sooner. While all kids continually develop, some do so by leaps and bounds.

Many parents, especially first-time parents, may not even realize their child's potential because they have no contemporaries to compare him to. Perhaps some other parents may appreciate the special gifts they perceive but not realize that potential giftedness can flourish if nurtured. Still others rush to buy or make flash cards, computer software, or expensive "educational" toys and games because they haven't time to read to the child.

Whatever the cause, for many years parents have overlooked ways they could optimize the development of their infants and toddlers. While all children benefit from proper balance and encouragement at every stage of development, our feeling is that children who show early signs of giftedness are especially in need of proper care to ensure balanced development. In the words of Burton White, "Relatively few families—perhaps no more than one in ten—manage to get their children through the age period from eight to thirty-six months as well educated and developed as they can and should be."

Lots of growth occurs in the busy months before a child's third birthday. There is for us no more reliable guide to the kind of development we should expect to see than Burton White's book, *The First Three Years of Life*. White and his associates have probably spent more hours with more toddlers than any other research team.

While Piaget formed his landmark opinions about the development of intelligence from watching his own children grow, White and his associates at the Center for Parent Education have spent tens of thousands of hours with thousands of children in their homes as well as

in lab settings. White's carefully trained observers spend time to become regular fixtures in the households they visit; they also are trained in nonintrusive technique so that life goes on without special behavior for the observer's sake.

The most significant product of this enormous mass of data is the identification of seven distinct phases in the development of infants. Knowing what phase your child is going through, and how to recognize when he's entering the next one, can be extremely helpful, especially to the parents of a first baby.

Phases one through five all are seen by the time an infant is 8 months old. This chapter deals with growth during White's period of phases six (8 to 14 months), seven (14 to 24 months), and eight (24 to 36 months). During this period, a substantial part of the development of the child's language abilities and self-concept take place. The period is also marked by insatiable curiosity and a sense of social awareness. Besides support and encouragement from his family, the toddler needs solid foundations for his moral development at this point, and he deserves a well-defined, disciplined view of his place in the world. If these last elements are ignored at this stage, the costs could be high later on when the promising child finds himself spoiled, friendless, lacking motivation, and discouraged by rejection.

CURIOSITY

Without hesitation, we suggest that curiosity is the key element in the emerging toddler. His insatiable need to know and grow take him to every corner. The bright toddler seems to teach himself to creep in order to find out what's behind the sofa, what's around the corner, what's in the book basket or toy box. "Nothing is more important for a child's educational development," writes Burton White in *The First Three Years of Life*, "than a well-developed curiosity."

If you are able to do nothing else during your child's infancy, be sure you give him every opportunity to learn from his curiosity. Don't build walls; open doors. Probably nothing else parents do is as important to the development of the child's intelligence.

Except for the gates that restrict him from areas that cannot be childproofed, he needs all the free rein he can get. Don't use restraints except when they are genuinely unavoidable: for example, when you're carrying groceries in from the car, carrying loads of wash to the basement, or transferring boiling water from stove to sink. Playpens are for brief utility in those situations, and shouldn't be used as checkrooms for fussy toddlers.

When away from home, the baby will fare better carried on your hip or in a front or back carrier. There he'll have more eye contact, more interaction with things and people, more processing of all he sees. You can keep a conversation going with him, and make detours to follow things you see have caught his eye.

"When I see a child strapped into a stroller," a mother told us, "I can't help but imagine an invalid confined to a wheelchair." She used the stroller minimally; otherwise she carried her toddlers on her hip.

Leave the stroller behind on short walks, too, if you can, and your baby will reap the benefit. You'll arrive a little later but more enriched. Take time, as the saying goes, to smell the flowers—and feel the bark, pick up a leaf, feed crumbs to the ants, and feel the sunshine. Infants, especially those inclined toward the higher ranges of intelligence, tend to be observant of small details and aware of changes from day to day or between seasons.

When you take a trip to the zoo, museum, or park with toddler and preschool children, try to see the sights from their level. Adults who pay admission fees tend to want to cover the most mileage for their money. Better to spend, say, ninety minutes in the children's petting area and come back another day to explore again. For little ones, sometimes less is more.

Remember that a child's right to indulge his curiosity ends where it begins to interfere with another's rights or property. Don't be afraid to set limits! "Those papers are you mother's and she needs them for something she's doing, so we can't draw on them. We'll get some drawing paper if you'd like to color." A distraction or redirection is much more effective than the word no.

Use no as a caution rather than a curtailment. Burton White points out that repeated overuse of the word no to a toddler who's exploring encourages him to associate curiosity with disapproval, which is the opposite of what we'd like him to feel. Distract or redirect. (Notice we didn't say to overlook inappropriate behavior because we told you to go easy on the word no.)

With gifted children even more than others, it's important to set up enforcement of limits when they're very young. Very bright children become quite skilled later at manipulating parents, outmaneuvering them and outdistancing them. Two intelligent parents are often outnumbered by one gifted child. All children need consistent limits at an early age, and you do your child no favor if you continually make exceptions and exemptions.

Be as flexible as possible but be firm and consistent with the rules you feel are necessary to enforce. If you can establish quiet and gentle authority at the toddler stage, you'll be spared a lot of grief later on. Because of his reasoning and motivating skills, he'll argue to the death on a small point if you let him.

BORN TO PLAY

Play is crucial for the gifted child's self-esteem. It is what distinguishes the concept of giftedness from that of the "superbaby." Play encouraged for its own sake enhances personal expression and encourages creative approaches to work in later life.

A toddler's exploration, so closely linked with his self-concept, should not be tied up by efforts on the part of parents to self-consciously create educational play. The child whose play is watched over incessantly and "stolen" by adults, who is dragged into "educational" games and activities, who is prevented from playing cops and robbers because of its violence, all the while being primed for preschool, is not being allowed to develop his giftedness any more than the child who is ignored by his parents.

Over the years we have heard of people who think gifted children can get along quite nicely on little bits of play, just as some of them need less sleep. Nothing could be farther from the truth. Benjamin Bloom and his associates at the University of Chicago recently published findings from a major retrospective study in their book, *Developing Talent in Young People*. They took acknowledged world-class talents in six fields who had grown up since the 1950s, and interviewed them and their parents, teachers, and coaches to find out what it was that got them through the maze of novices to the top of their professions. Again and again these people said their first exposure to their talent area was casual and playful. Their first teachers typically were chosen for warmth and friendliness, not for their talent, virtuosity, or perfectionism. Early lessons were full of smiles and encouragement.

Learning in a child's first year is channeled directly through play. The more stimulation he gets during that play—more places, more playmates, more varied experiences—the broader his base of understanding, that is, his foundation for learning. The fact that it's crucial to his growth doesn't mean it shouldn't be fun.

For first hand proof, watch a toddler. Every time he learns a new trick he's delighted. It's fun to have a new skill. When a primary school student learns cursive writing, you can't *get* him to print for a long time. Once he's mastered balancing on a two-wheeler, he doesn't want to be caught dead on a bike with training wheels.

In a sense parents are the child's first playmates, and even his first toys. They're most effective when they provide a variety of experiences and learning opportunities, stepping in from time to time when it's necessary but not trying to mold the child's thoughts.

Play can be an end in itself, as work should be. It is self-expression, a vehicle for the development of critical and creative thinking, of inductive and deductive reasoning, of manipulating symbols that a child masters before moving out into the complex outside world.

When infants first manage to creep around, they gravitate toward hinged items, balls, and other small portable devices. Stacking and nesting toys and sorting devices fascinate them. Solving the mystery of their use is a joy.

The parents' role at this point is to provide a rich experiential environment. Opportunities for creative play are important, but expect more mess than art and more noise than music. Good, harmonious music in the home lays the groundwork for a firm footing in music, just as rich language and interesting colors and patterns provide good background in the language and visual arts. Blocks, clay, and finger paints have their place as the child toddles past his first birthday.

Most children love to play with basic rhythm instruments and art media. Having a regular place to display artwork helps the child's developing self-image. Use one effort as a springboard to another outlet: let a picture inspire a song, a song inspire a dance, and so on.

When your child brings you a work of art ask him to tell you about it. Write the narrative on the paper. Next, have him dictate the story of a trip or a special event on drawing paper and let him illustrate it.

Remember that creativity is a blessing. Kids begin to draw abstractly, and we systematically beat it out of them till they are rubber-stamp realists. Give them credit. One 4-year-old drew some classic emerging human figures—all round head with two stick legs descending from the chin and two stick arms radiating out of what should have been the ears. She studied it for a while, then hunkered down till her knees were next to her chin, hunched her shoulders up as high as she could, stuck her arms straight out, mimicked a wide-eyed smiley face, and said: "Look, Dad—here's how I draw people." As Woody Allen asked, "Does art mirror life, or what?"

Imagination gets trimmed too. Kids have wonderful appreciation for fantasy, which can sometimes be hampered in the name of realism. Better harnessed than hobbled.

Pretending or make-believe play may surface around the first birthday. Burton White reports in *The First Three Years of Life* that such play is especially common in unusually competent children, and should be encouraged by parents. Make- believe brings new dimensions to play; it's like giving a child's mind stretching exercises just as a runner stretches his leg muscles during warm-up for a marathon. Let your chldren act zany, dress in mismatched clothes, and take flights of whimsey when they feel so moved.

Toys should encourage action, respond to action, and be versatile. Toys are a catalyst, a means rather than an end. Games allow children to analyze, synthesize, and evaluate within rules or guidelines while relating to adults, especially parents. Alphabet and number puzzles are a good way to familiarize a child with those abstract elements.

One mother found that her toddler was ready to move beyond the simple wooden puzzles, but was a little intimidated by the much larger ones. Her solution was to skip the outline frame; she got a piece of cardboard the same size and traced around the pieces with a heavy marker—just enough help to allow him to do the puzzle himself.

Toddlers develop a keen sense of smell and taste when you let them help in the kitchen. They can knead bread dough, decorate cookies, frost cakes, though again you can expect more of a mess than actual assistance. Helping you measure out ingredients is wonderful preparation for math, and the change in form your creations go through lay groundwork for understanding chemistry.

Infants will start with a fascination for opening and closing books, and bright colors will entertain them enormously. Toddlers continue to be fascinated by books and begin to show an interest in stories. By age 2 many gifted toddlers are ready for more complex stories. One girl's parents were surprised by one gift she received for her second birthday, one of Beatrix Potter's longest books, *The Tale of Mr. Tod*. It was short on action and long on description. But to their surprise, the child couldn't get enough of it, asking that it be read aloud to her over and over—at about twenty minutes per pass.

Your children will associate books and reading with the love that they feel surrounded by as you play and share and spend time with them. The time and sharing is the central point; specific titles or reading programs are secondary. Play, above all else, is self-motivation, and development of that quality is key to the growth of a hale and hearty gifted child.

Shop for children's books that convey a sense of delight through their subjects, their artwork, their language, and how they lend themselves to being read aloud. (Later we describe several books, authors, and publishers who are doing marvelous work.) Don't worry if the books aren't about quantum mechanics or wave dynamics. There's time for that, and plenty of books for that purpose. Help your child love books, and he'll eventually find books on the subjects he grows to love. If he sees you turning to books for answers, enlightenment, inspiration, and entertainment, he'll follow.

Speaking of questions—ask questions of each other sometimes as you read and tell stories. Encourage the child to participate and to think. What *other* ending to the story would be plausible? What would *you* do in this situation? Books are made by people who began as readers; your child may imagine as good or better a resolution of a story line as the author. This exercise also plants a seed of truth in your young child's mind: This book was written by somebody, and I'm somebody; therefore I could write a book.

These questions can lead anywhere. The gifted 2-year-old often expresses his curiosity through endless questions. No matter how many and how often, *do not lose your cool*. Cheer up; in ten or twelve years he probably won't even talk to you. Meanwhile, every question deserves an interested response. You are not required to know everything.

All children ask questions. What makes gifted children different is they will wait six or eight months, ask the same question, and challenge you if you give a different answer. Plead the Fifth Amendment. They will ask you tougher questions too. What's beyond outer space? If we invented a universal solvent, where would we keep it? If genders are equal why did God make woman second? ("If at first you don't succeed . . ." answered one gifted girl.) How come Scotch tape doesn't stick to the roll or the machine that made it? Why is the sky blue?

These are important questions, and they deserve careful answers. If you don't have a degree in engineering and the physical sciences, find a book with a somewhat ambiguous title, *High Tech Babies*, by Emily Williams. In it she gives simple, concise answers to common questions about the world around us.

Williams also quotes a book by Marianne Besser, *Growing Up with Science*:

> Besser interviewed the parents of the Science Talent Search winners, high school students who, in the late 1950s, showed extraordinary talent in the area of science and mathematics. When the parents were asked how they felt they had contributed to the development of their child's talent during his or her early years, these parents consistently pointed to the same thing—a tendency to reward their children's earliest questions with interest and with answers. Their children were encouraged to investigate and explore interesting objects and events to whatever extent they wanted, within the realms of safety. From their children's earliest years, these parents had placed a high premium on finding out why, and extending the investigations to the farthest limits.

Whenever it is possible, then, allow the toddler to see, touch, experience the answer. When you don't know the answer, offer to find out. Even a 2-year-old will enjoy the trip to a library to look up information.

LANGUAGE DEVELOPMENT

Some—*but by no means all*—gifted children speak early. Einstein is the most notorious exception to this rule; he didn't speak until he was 4 years old nor read until he was 7. It's generally accepted that he caught up.

More important than spoken vocabulary is *receptive language*, the words the infant understands and acts upon. Months before she says anything back, your infant may understand brief sentences such as "Wave bye," or "Give Daddy a hug," or even "Bring me a book and I'll read to you." Even when the child isn't saying a word, what she hears, processes, and acts upon may in fact speak volumes. According to Arthur Guilford, Jane Scheuerle, and Susan Shonbrun, all from the University of South Florida, in "Aspects of Language Development in the Gifted," *Gifted Child Quarterly*, Vol. 25, No. 4, Fall 1981, p. 159:

"Among the various elements of early language, receptive vocabulary is reported to have the highest correlation to intellectual ability."

This is why we urge you to talk with your children every day of their lives—notice we don't say every moment. An hour without silence would be like the type on this page without borders. The dramatist knows the eloquence of silence; the city planner knows the value of open space. Too much of a good thing can lead to system shutdown.

Parents of "late" talkers are often surprised when their child's first words come in a complete sentence. There is a joke about a little boy who never spoke until he was almost 5, when at the dinner table he turned to his mother and said, "You really burned the meat loaf tonight." Aghast, she replied, "Why, honey, you never talked before!" He shrugged it off, saying, "You never burned the meat loaf before."

Meat loaf notwithstanding, Burton White in *Educating the Infant and Toddler* reports that first receptive language is processed and used between 8 and 10 months of age, first spoken words may come anywhere from 8 to 18 months, which is really a wide range. While it's not clear what the exact relationship is between language acuity and intellectual ability, it's easy to see that a child with good command of language would score high on the language-loaded IQ tests. With that ability would come a greater tendency to be identified as "gifted" than his peers whose talents are nonverbal or less easily targeted by tests.

Dr. White extracted subjects from his research who were later found to have well-developed language skills. Correlating his associates' notes, he summarizes these teaching styles observed among the parents of those children:

1. The child usually initiated about ten interchanges an hour with her parents. Parents initiated slightly fewer (and fewer still with second or third children).
2. Parents took the time to identify the interest of the child.
3. Words and appropriate actions, focused on the child's interest, usually followed.
4. Words were at or slightly above the child's apparent level of comprehension.
5. Full sentences, rather than single words or brief phrases, were the norm.
6. Related ideas were introduced often.
7. Most interchanges lasted between twenty and thirty seconds. Lengthy teaching sessions were rare.
8. Stories were read often, but the child's attention did not become sustained until well into the second year. For a few months after the child's first birthday, picture books were used habitually for "label-

ing" sessions—that is, a chance to point at a picture of a ball, a bunny, or a boat.

Regarding the last point concerning attention span, many parents of gifted children attest that an uncommonly long attention span was an early sign of their children's abilities. One 9-month-old wanted to hear the Mother Goose rhymes read over and over every morning before she got out of bed. Her brother, just after his first birthday, would sit enthralled if read to for two or three hours at a time.

GROWTH OF POSITIVE SELF-CONCEPT

Good intellectual curiosity and strong language skills, when both are present, give a child exceptionally good footing from which to launch the development of his talents. But all this is small consolation if the child has somehow failed to develop a positive self-concept along the way.

Initially the infant sees the caretaker as an extension of himself. Then gradually he begins to make a distinction—drawing a line where he ends and the caretaker begins. As these concepts emerge the parents must communicate a sense of respect for the infant as an individual, but at the same time building in a mutual respect for themselves.

Beginnings of self-concept relate to the development of trust in the primary caretaker in the first months of life.

This applies to intellectual development as well. "Let the child find joy in learning and sense of curiosity and inquisitiveness," said one teacher who is also the mother of a gifted child. "This would eliminate problems in older children. They could better be themselves."

Starting at about 3 months of age, one gifted child who developed a good self-concept was exposed to the outdoors and allowed to investigate an environment created to allow sensory perceptions for him. Starting at 8 months he was taken for walks, carried so he could see everything in front of him. At 18 months, he had his own garden plot to dig in and began interacting with animals—pets such as fish and crabs. He was given an opportunity to participate in all his parents' activities; he used body language to inquire about things around him; he used big words. As a toddler he would go to the park daily and into shops, quickly learning his surroundings and where he could go.

"He had a good self-concept because he never felt limited," his mother explains. "His love for animals and plants helped him to develop a reverence for life and respect for others."

How different an upbringing from that of a 2-year-old boy Barbara Clark described in her book, *Growing Up Gifted*. He was

> sitting in a garden watching a little "bug" move slowly across the ground. The child was fascinated by the fact that the little thing had so many legs yet still was able to move without falling down. . . . There was hair all over its legs.
>
> Just then an amazing thing happened. The bug jumped. It jumped up onto a nearby leaf, and, of all things, it spit threads out of its back end. The child had seen people spit, but never had he seen anything spit out of its back end. He watched this happen again and again. Then, to his disbelief, the thing walked on its own spit! Well, this was getting to be too much. Someone in the house was missing all of this. She was such a nice, fun person, and he loved her very much; yet she couldn't see and share it all with him. He knew she wouldn't be able to come out there into the garden. He just wanted her to see it, just for a minute. Happily, he picked it up and started toward the house. He went right to his mother and held his treasure up high for her to see.
>
> As he left the house to return the "nasty, dirty, horrible, ugly spider" to its place in the garden, he thought about what she had just said. She must be right, she was always right; he knew that. Well if she was right, then he must be wrong.

"We were born with a center core—our essence—that is unique to us and is our real self," writes Clark.

> Tiny babies have no problem communicating to us the real needs or desires they feel. Expressing the real self is never a problem at the beginning. But, as the child in the garden discovered, it does not take long before other information causes us to doubt the messages from our center core. After enough dissonant information enters our awareness, a shell begins to build around this lovely, real center, and it is made up of all the "crummy" stuff we feel and believe about ourself after encounters like these.

The intelligence and sensitivity of gifted children make them especially susceptible to poor images of themselves, partly because of their own high expectations about themselves.

The precocity of the gifted toddler may be misinterpreted. High expectations are acquired before some social skills. For example, another gifted girl naturally took responsibility for others, regardless of their age.

She understood what everybody *should* be doing. Her moral sense was accurate, but her targets didn't always appreciate being set straight. Shy upon meeting new friends, she would offer free moral advice once she felt more familiar. Her awareness of order and fairness preceded her social adroitness.

Here is a good example of how a gifted child's outer behavior can send the wrong signals to adults who are used to working with normal infants and toddlers. Another girl was almost 3 when her nursery school staff said she was a discipline problem and in need of help. She was overly independent and unruly, they said, and had an aggressive personality; she caused trouble and bullied other children at school. When tested, the behavioral "problem" turned out to be a symptom of her profound giftedness; she was already bored literally to distraction and tears by her age-mates.

Her parents found themselves in a classic situation: their child wasn't fitting in well, so a teacher labeled her as a behavior-disordered pupil. We know this misdiagnosis is not uncommon in primary and secondary grades. Fortunately it opened other doors: The girl is thriving in a full-time school for gifted children, where she feels more normal and teachers have insights into working with kids like her. We hope the child's parents were quick to remind the girl of their own and others' high regard for her.

SOCIAL AND MORAL DEVELOPMENT

There is a direct link between the emergence of self-concept and the child's developing social skills and moral makeup. For the infant the world community is his family; in its comfort and protection he must learn the rudiments of social behavior: cooperation, respect, taking turns, and sacrificing individual wants for common needs. These rules of behavior are absolutely essential, and if they are not acquired in the first few years of life, they might never be learned later on. We don't have to look far to find examples of children who haven't caught on to where they fit into the larger scheme of things.

Families have an adjustment period during which children discover their own independence. If unprepared, parents can find themselves hurtling downhill without a steering wheel or brakes. Children discover that two-letter word no, and then the fun begins.

It helps to consider the child's roller coaster emotions as his emerging self comes head to head with the rest of the universe. As an infant his universe was a series of concentric rings with himself in the center. As a toddler he notices that sometimes he has to postpone gratification, share the things he loves most (including parents if a sibling arrives on the scene), and he may feel that his concentric rings are really a target, and the center he's standing in is in fact the bull's-eye.

Balance is the essential element in this period of growth. The child needs to know that his rage doesn't destroy the objects it focuses on, especially when he imagines that destruction might be a solution to his momentary frustrations. He needs reassurance that the world can withstand his attacks, that his parents can endure his terrorism, and that he is secure in his family setting even though his behavior may be temporarily unacceptable. What he doesn't need is the feeling that there are no consequences to his behavior; that he can and should manipulate his environment and all who dwell therein; or that tantrums replace negotiation.

Any child who fails to be given that balanced perspective can become a liability to his community, regardless of the promise or potential he also carries. The parent who neglects to impart a proper balance within the family fails the child. The child who fails to learn social behavior will not be accepted, or effective, within his community—as a child or as an adult.

A recent book, *The Too Precious Child*, by Lynne Williams, Henry S. Berman, and Louisa Rose, deals with what happens to children who remain the center of their universe. For any number of reasons, these children somehow become "too precious children." Some may be the only children of an older professional couple, who have focused all their latent parenting aspirations on the success of this one effort. Other kids become "too precious" because they survive accidents, injury, divorce, or disease. Another "at-risk" group are the gifted. However they get that way, the result of being "too precious" is that they are excused from obligations to contribute to society or treat others respectfully; they don't have to make their beds or get to school on time; if their homework isn't finished their parents will call the teacher to ask for an extension. Their trespasses are always forgiven. They thus are exempted from the law of natural consequences.

Sometimes these kids are helpless victims of the Too Precious Syndrome—like the violinist who isn't allowed to play baseball because his fingers might get hurt; the talented child whose stage mother hustles her from audition to vocal coach to dance class; the child of joint custody who gets hopelessly doted on by both parents. Even Olympic-hopeful figure skaters can do dishes, mow lawns, and take the garbage out. Talent isn't an exemption from responsibility; if anything, it mandates acceptance of responsibility.

The gifted child has no less a need to learn his part in the scheme of things; he has an equal stake in his community, and one day may feel an inspiration to take part in shaping its future.

The gifted child often has a heightened sensitivity to the feelings of others and a greater awareness of his own emotions. With guidance he can learn to identify and label emotions and perceive them in others from clues such as body language. One family used the kitchen blackboard to write, "Kate is ANGRY" when their 2-year-old bordered on a temper tantrum. She would take the eraser and remove "angry" when the feeling had subsided, asking that "happy" be written in its place. She seemed to be making her emotions tangible and manageable.

Just as the child "invents" his own structure of language and rules of basic math, he will construct a system of moral sense from the behavior he observes. Piaget holds that all knowledge is constructed in this way, and that play is constructive in demonstrating relationships from which the child develops his own order of knowledge. How else could a 2-year-old construct a complex sentence? You couldn't teach him the complex rules of order that allow him to say, "I put it in the little red box by the door," but by listening to patterns of speech around him he "knows" enough to do it. When he constructs according to his perception of the rules of grammar we often find the result amusing—as, "There's him," or "I brang you a cookie." This kind of usage is the direct product of original thought process, not just imitation.

So, it is held, does the child form his own structured view of social issues: the way people treat each other, age relationships, gender roles, and how families work. Undertaking activities such as washing dolls of different skin color, interviewing other children about their families, hearing people talk about their work, and visiting other homes may stimulate questions that lead to the formulation of structured knowledge.

Can we help that kind of development? Yes, and we do so passively every day without realizing it. How do we do so intentionally? Subtly, it is hoped. Nudge the process with an indirect question, or materials rearranged, or by posing a conflicting viewpoint, perhaps as a "what if" scenario. This is also called "guided reinvention" of knowledge.

Can this kind of learning be encouraged in the classroom? Yes, and Dr. Carolyn Edwards, in her *Promoting Moral and Social Development in Young Children*, observes that

> the whole domain of social-cognitive research should serve as a starting point for a more holistic Piagetian approach to education. . . . It is central to the child because when a teacher moves away from an instructional and directive role and allows the child to construct knowledge freely, the child gets the biggest possible boost in becoming a self-initiated thinker and discoverer. When both adults and children use initiative in thinking about social and moral issues, they begin to construct knowledge autonomously in all domains.
>
> Development is not the result of maturation unfolding from within the child. Nor is it the result of a simple copying of the environment outside the child. Rather, it is the result of interaction between child and the environment, regulated by the child.

What kinds of activities bring these principles to younger children? According to Dr. Carolyn Edwards, for awareness of age groups and roles, use dolls representing various ages or photos grouped by age or sequence on wall displays. To dramatize relationships with age groups, tape photos of people of various ages to toy phones, and let the child "talk" to each person, making appropriate changes in subject or language level. Three-year-olds can discuss things that people of varying ages can and can't do. They can visit newborn babies and nursing homes, and label or sort photographs of people of various age ranges. They can cut pictures of people from magazines, group them, and arrange them into posters or booklets.

Development of self-concept is directly related to moral development, for a child's vision of self not only reflects treatment by others but is expressed in treatment of others as well. A study of gifted 3- year-olds by Kippy Abroms and Joan Gollin of Tulane University ("Developmental Study of Gifted Preschool Children and Measures of Psychosocial Giftedness," *Exceptional Children*, Vol. 6, No. 5, 1980) indicated that "psychosocial giftedness . . . may develop somewhat independently of IQ and cognitive role taking." Thus, qualities of leadership and high moral development may not be guaranteed by a child's giftedness, but

"prosocial" behaviors can be encouraged in the preschool years by "structure, modeling and the use of positive reinforcement. . . . Creative role play appears to be well suited for igniting awareness and a broad range of interpersonal effects resulting from one's own behavior." Thus we help the child recognize others' rights and perspectives.

Dr. Edwards describes how a teacher can use a skit with a group of preschoolers or an interview with one student to present a story-situation posing a social-cognitive problem. The story-situation becomes a cognitive conflict requiring resolution. The teacher invites discussion and asks questions to encourage a closer look at the underlying moral or social problems involved in the situation. The teacher does not provide answers of judgment but encourages the children to think about constructing their own values. Such an approach can easily be adapted for home use by a parent using puppets or make-believe role-playing. The child gains in self-confidence and self-respect as well as in moral development through this approach.

Discipline

Discipline requires knowing what is developmentally appropriate for a child and what is consistent with his mental ability, and seeking responses appropriate to the occasion.

Simple rules such as "You may not hurt yourself or anyone else" and "You may not destroy objects" are sufficient to cover most discipline problems that arise. Consequences must be a logical extension of the problem or promote thinking. Spilled milk generally is not a discipline problem but a maturational motor problem. Spilled milk cleaned up by the child teaches that one is responsible for his action more readily than words. After the first few months, and particularly from 15 to 22 months when many children are testing the limits of behavior, persistent setting of limits is important, with follow-through that removes temptations rather than just making idle threats.

Parents mentioned simple rules, such as the Golden Rule and the Ten Commandments, as being used to guide children's behavior and give explanations of proper behavior. "If basic human traits are not adhered to, a person will not feel right with himself," one mother explained.

When considering appropriate discipline to enforce consistent rules and reinforce a child's self-concept, consider physical proximity, intervention, and logical consequences. An adult being near a child may be enough to change behavior. Intervention can involve teaching of social and verbal skills that lead to an explanation of logical consequences.

Another parent said he used a specially designated chair as a place for a "time-out" to discipline toddlers—though not for a long period and always with an explanation to the child of why the behavior had been unacceptable. Always aim to treat and correct misbehavior positively, avoiding use of negative language.

While keeping lecturing to a minimum, discipline can be an opportunity for encouraging the child to develop higher-level thinking skills such as analysis, synthesis, and evaluation, rather than "mindless" punishment.

At first reading, presiding over the growth of a toddler may seem an enormous task. Just remember that it gets easier after the first five or six kids. (One mother who found her third and fourth children less stressful as infants allowed that "the first two should be considered throwaways," but we're not endorsing that view.) Be encouraged as well as challenged: these are the critical years, and the importance of the investment you make at this time cannot be overestimated. "To me it's like money in the bank," wrote one mother. "You can't withdraw if you don't deposit first. You have to build yourself a well-established account to keep your credit and balance good. Then if you need it, it will be there."

3

The Preschool Years

Somewhere between the third birthday and the first day of school the emerging person peeks out from behind the Oshkosh coveralls, looks around, likes what he sees, puts on new shoes, and steps out into the world with confidence. Some of this happens overnight. Tasks that he recently needed help for he's doing by himself. The questions still come, but they are more insightful and require a bit more thought and sometimes more elaborate answers.

By the same token, the evidences of his special gifts become more concrete, sometimes clustering around certain characteristics or abilities. Here are some of the behaviors, abilities, and tendencies you might notice:

The gifted preschooler:
Likes to "play" with words
Uses proper grammar and structure earlier than age-mates
Uses rich language with colorful metaphor or analogy
Stops to ask about new words, learns them, and practices using them
Shows long attention span for stories or conversations, and can accurately retell stories with details

Learns to read, without being taught, before starting school
Comes up with unusual or clever responses to questions
Has keen sense of humor
Is very independent
Makes up stories, songs, or rhymes
Fantasizes readily

May have imaginary playmates

Understands complex concepts and issues like death, time, God, ethical questions of right and wrong
Infers cause-and-effect relationship of parts, intuits how things work
Asks probing questions and genuinely wants to hear and process the answers
Shows interest and skill in classifying things
Collects unusual items and learns all he can about them

Demonstrates leadership abilities
Is sensitive to feelings of others
Reads body language
Generates varied and interesting play situations
Adapts to needs or skill levels of playmates
Modifies his language level for less mature children
Can emphathize with relative abilities of the handicapped
Uses verbal skills to deal with conflicts or influence other children

Understands counting with one-to-one correspondence
Does some calculations in his head
Enjoys ordering, cataloguing, grouping, arranging by sequence or gradation
Learns value of coins, understands how to make change
Shows strong interest in time concepts, clocks, and calendars
Puts puzzles together with facility

Can sing in tune or match the pitch of a note played or sung
Can listen to two short melodies and tell whether they are the same or different
Learns notes and words to simple songs quickly and easily, with a minimum of repetition

Remembers things he has seen accurately and in great detail
Shows unusual skill in art activities
Uses material or media in original ways; shows distinctive techniques and style

May draw a correct floor plan of a room from memory

Can remember landmarks and turns on the way to familiar places
Can visualize from the basement which room is overhead
Immediately notices small changes in furnishings or furniture arrangement; hair style, eyeglass frames, or new clothing of family or friends

Connects memories with present happenings
Remembers and carries out complex instructions involving several steps
Applies something learned in one field or experience with some other area of life
Takes an example from a story or shared experience and applies it to his life
Takes things like phones and clocks apart

Develops a sense of order and notices changes from routine
May resist change
Has a high energy level, needing less sleep than age-mates
Has older playmates and enjoys speaking with adults

Resents unfairness
Doesn't want his things moved or rearranged
Is intolerant of disorder or contrary conclusions
Sees many sides of a question, tolerates ambiguity well, even to the point of having difficulty with true/false hypotheses
Builds on experiences to get a broader perspective

Has intense powers of concentration and persists at tasks
Exhibits perfectionism
Learns new material rapidly; easily masters new skills or topics

THE IMPORTANCE OF BALANCE

You will notice that we've loaded these traits liberally with qualifiers: your child *may* this and *might* that. This is because there are dozens of subtle signs you'll pick up along the way. If you're watching for all of them, you may spot signs in more than one area. If your child is good at math, she might also shine in music. If her language skills are strong, maybe her creativity and leadership are also strong.

There is a considerable danger of the prodigy effect—the "first star I see tonight" syndrome. When you first see signs of exceptional music or math ability you may feel tempted to rent Carnegie Hall or apply to MIT. Keep your options open for *all* your child's potential. Don't specialize too early.

Keep things in balance during the preschool years. Properly encouraged, the first talent you notice will continue to develop with the child's own natural ambition to do more of what she likes and does best. Be sure she has lots of exposure to other skills and talents, because there may be a second star of even greater magnitude lurking behind the flash of the first one. Moreover, the gifted child has a better chance of being accepted in her community if she's well rounded in many areas. Not the best in everything, but *competent*.

If your child is always the last eliminated in spelling bees, but also the last chosen for softball teams, he and all the other kids will know it. That can be a double whammy: two excuses for shunning him. If, on the other hand, he holds his own in right field, it's so much easier for the other kids to "forgive" his giftedness. No need to star, mind you, just fall comfortably within the midthird of typical athletic ability.

Moreover, many gifted children are advanced intellectually but are below age level in motor skills and social/emotional development, leading to peer problems in school.

The preschool years are the time when you should measure and can supplement the balance of skills and talents. Give him every kind of stimulus, find out what he can do well, and as he goes full tilt into his favorite things, remember to encourage him to explore others as well.

Parents who love books tend to generate kids who love books. So far so good. But parents who are long on language skills may not recognize a preschooler's propensity for math. Even when they do, they might not have the faintest idea of how to lay a foundation in a field they're not familiar with—math or music, for example. They may pass along their voids instead of filling the gaps.

At the end of this chapter we offer a section of idea starters for activities you can dovetail into your daily routine. For the most part they

use everyday household objects that most people have on hand. We also include a resource list, with some of the best books we've uncovered.

Where else to turn for help? Libraries, YMCAs, gyms, schools, story hours, play groups, park districts, garage sales, mail-order catalogues, basements, forests, and—who knows?—maybe even television. Television *used properly* is one of the joys of our time—as a teacher, *not* as a baby-sitter.

Another joy of our time, considerably less celebrated at this point but that could be as far-reaching in the development of preschoolers, is a program developed by Burton White and his associates and the state of Missouri in the Ferguson-Florissant and three other Missouri school districts.

Based in part on Dr. White's work at the Center for Parent Education in Massachusetts, the Parents as Teachers program is an ambitious project to equip new parents for their role as early educators from birth through infancy and the important first years of life. White and parent-educator colleagues enabled parents to recognize the stages of develop-ment in their babies, while watching for developmental anomalies and screening for learning disabilities or difficulties. Their hope was to equip parents with the skills and materials to enhance their children's develop-ment while screening for problems that might lead to learning dis-abilities during the school years.

Results of the pilot program were gratifying, and the state has man-dated its use in all districts. It may be a while before its full effects are felt and measured, but this program may well be the first full and official step toward supporting parents in their role as first teachers across the country.

Meanwhile, it has already yielded a number of significant con-clusions, both to school system administrators with hundreds of thousands of students and to parents with one infant; the application of these findings is no less significant for either.

Here are parts of the evaluation report from the state of Missouri:

- PAT children scored significantly higher on all measures of intel-ligence, achievement, auditory comprehension, verbal ability and language ability than did comparison children.
- PAT children demonstrated significantly more aspects of positive social development . . . able to distinguish a "self" identity, to have positive adult relations, and to have coping capabilities.

- Parents were more knowledgeable about physical stimuli . . . about discipline, and about child development.
- PAT children identified as potentially "at risk" for traditional socioeconomic reasons—parent's age, education, income, single-parents households, or large numbers of siblings—performed as well as non-risk children. However, children judged by NPAT staff as "at risk" because of family stress, delayed gross motor development, and inappropriate behavior consistently performed more poorly on all measures of intelligence, achievement, and language development than did children who were not observed to be "at risk."
- The higher PAT staff rated the quality of parent participation in the PAT study, the better the children performed on all testing measures.
- The greater the frequency of parent participation in home visits, the more likely were children to demonstrate positive aspects of social development, include pride in their accomplishment and capability for expressing emotions. Parents who attended group meetings with greater frequency were more knowledgeable about the importance of physical stimuli and hearing/motor development knowledge.
- PAT parents were more likely to regard their school district as responsive to their child's needs than were parents of non-participating children.
- Nearly all PAT parents reported a high degree of satisfaction with each of the project services, including group meetings, private home visits and screenings. Almost all parents felt that project services made a difference in the way they perceived their parenting role.

The impact of these findings can be enormous for state systems and homes alike. Although the program was aimed at full development of all young children with an eye to identifying and correcting any physical impairments to learning before the children reached school age, it is significant that all children in the project showed higher intelligence, achievement, and language development when their parents engaged in an active, instructed program of parenting. We choose to draw a parallel in households where potentially gifted children are the product; we believe the parents have a sizeable role in the proper development of those talents or gifts.

More information by Drs. Meyeroff and White on the nature of the project is available in the September, 1986, issue of *Psychology Today*, which many local libraries display. Dr. White evaluated the program at length in his *Educating the Infant and Toddler*, a D. C. Heath book that may be ordered from booksellers or accessed through interlibrary loan.

Moreover, the materials developed jointly by the Center for Parent Education and the Fergusson-Florissant school district are available by mail to parents and schools alike. Write to request a listing of early education materials from Early Education Programs, Ferguson-Florissant School District, 1005 Waterford Drive, Florissant, MO 63033.

While the project was never intended to identify the gifted population headed toward school registration, the materials developed for the program are available and extremely useful to all parents. Booklets detail recommended activities for children from birth through age 5. Those for the preschool range include such topics as: "Home Activities for 3's and 4's"; "Discovery for 4's and 5's"; "Developing Creativity"; "Exploring Math Experiences"; and "Motor Development for 3's to 5's."

These materials can be kept on hand and brought out when your child first indicates that she's ready for them. If your child is developing earlier than others around her, this information will help you compare her timing with the normal range. If you're not particularly stellar in some area of development, these pamphlets will give you activities and approaches to help balance her overall performance.

Keep in mind that children progress at individual rates and don't always swim in schools like minnows. The range for the first appearance of some behaviors, for example, extends a full year. That means there's no need to watch your child with a calendar and a stopwatch. No anxiety should be provoked by these tables of data; it's not appropriate, and it gets in the way of loving, caring, confident parenting.

Another useful set of materials available to parents comes from the Institute for Child Behavior and Development at the University of Illinois in Champaign-Urbana. For several decades Dr. Merle B. Karnes, director, has pioneered and spearheaded volumes of research and materials that help teachers educate handicapped, talented and gifted children.

Materials developed over a ten-year period (1975–86) for Project RAPYHT (Retrieval and Acceleration of Promising Young Handicapped and Talented) have been adapted for a new program geared toward identifying and developing giftedness in disadvantaged preschoolers involved in federally funded Project Head Start.

Funded in part by the U.S. Department of Health and Human Services through its Office of Human Development Services, the new materials are called BOHST: Bringing Out Head Start Talents. The BOHST materials give parents and teachers an orderly, step-by-step, hands-on method for identifying strong points in children's intellectual, motor, and talent development.

Beginning with assessment checklists and guidelines for identifying giftedness, these materials point the way to areas parents might wish to pursue, whether to encourage existing strengths or to round out areas where the child might need extra attention to become well-rounded.

At-Home Activities booklets, for example, each focus on developing one of the following talent areas: intellectual, creative, leadership, art, music, reading, math, science, and psychomotor. Each one costs one dollar. They are 12-page spiral bound booklets which include activities, things to do, places to go, and gift ideas to keep the processes going.

But the unqualified hit, for us, among the materials is the General Programming of thinking skills. Based on J. P. Guilford's Structure of the Intellect model, children are taught to think in three ways: convergent productive thinking, deductive productive thinking, and evaluative thinking. These modes of thought are personified in three animal mascots: Delores Detective, Ivan the Inventor, and Julius the Judge. The children hear stories about each of these mascots describing the methods each character uses in solving problems and the characteristics that made them good at their respective kinds of thinking.

A number of scripted exercises allow the introduction of each kind of thinking, and then provide the basis for spinoff exercises. This 286-page work costs less than $13. In this kit are posters of Delores Detective, Ivan the Inventor, and Julius the Judge. As an adult leads them through the exercises, children learn to choose when divergent, convergent or evaluative thinking might help them with tasks and situations they come up against. Take Delores:

> Delores Detective has certain qualities that make her a very clever detective. She's careful about examining all the available clues. She's patient about not jumping to the wrong conclusion. Even when she is baffled and doesn't know the answer, she hangs in there, pondering the question over and over in her mind. Once Delores has the scent, she'll keep thinking until she finds the solution to the mystery.

For example, the children pretend they're aboard a bus. From clues they pick up in scripted conversation, they try to guess the occupations of the speakers. In another, the teacher gives increasingly specific clues as they try to identify animals she describes. When a child guesses wrong, the response is, "That's a good guess, but it's not the one I'm thinking of."

Another workbook is devoted to talent programming, and includes group activities in the areas mentioned in the at-home activities booklets described above. Many of these can be adapted to individual use at home, as well.

All materials, as well as an order form describing them, are available from the Disabled Citizens Foundation, 1304 W. Bradley, Champaign, IL 61821.

Parents of gifted students consistently report that many of these children walked unsupported, talked, cut teeth, and otherwise progressed "earlier than normal." These developmental milestones were *among* but not necessarily the sole indicators of their child's exceptional abilities. Without building false expectations, then, we suggest that the appearance of one or more signs of early development *may* indicate the presence of potential giftedness, and in any event justify a close watch and gentle encouragement (*not* a push). And once again we drop the other shoe: absence of *any* signs of earlier-than-normal development does *not* rule out giftedness.

Now let's talk about what is, after all, normal.

The Missouri/White study produced a helpful chart, "Ages and Stages of Motor Development," which is a reliable and fair yardstick to use for ages 18 months to 6 years, one that allows for bracketing of ranges. Another, beginning at birth and continuing through the third birthday, was developed earlier by White for *The First Three Years of Life.*

As you begin to compare your child's behavior with these "normal" matrices, it's most important to keep track of what he does when. Not only will you find it helpful for comparison later, or for regaling him when he's 15, but it may provide strong supportive evidence if you're seeking early admission to school or admittance to a special gifted program. Include insightful remarks, use of elaborate language, or examples of advanced motor skills.

Please remember, we're not advocating early admission to school as a panacea. Later on you may feel it's the best solution for your child. We discuss the pros and cons of that option in a later chapter.

Early admission may be a means to an end, which should be to produce a young person who is at ease with herself, copes with and contributes to society, and is well grounded in the skills that will one day enable her to be a competent person.

At ages 3 and 4, children begin dealing with questions of self-concept, self-esteem, and morality. On the whole, gifted children don't have more problems with self-esteem than others. But they *can* have special difficulties if they feel "different" from other children as they socialize with peers and as they come to grips with their own talents and desire for perfection.

In *Roeper Review*, Nov. 1983, Reuben Altman, professor of special education at the University of Missouri in Columbia, speculates that self-esteem problems among gifted children may stem from these characteristics:

- A tendency toward critical thinking about themselves
- Exposure to older peers and their problems
- Earlier language development and earlier stress from self-evaluation
- Earlier developmental stages
- Awareness of being different

Parents can help their children learn to accept their differences as positive parts of their personality. These kids need to know that their divergent interests and learning styles are valid, even though they depart from the mainstream.

Consider the perfectionism and heightened sensitivity often found in gifted children. Don't tell the perfectionist to lower her acceptance threshold and settle for less. Rather, help her place her feelings and abilities in perspective.

Take, for example, the preschooler who is frustrated because he wants to draw in finer detail than his hands can execute. This is not the time to tell him that the drawing he made was great, because he knows it isn't. Instead you can make him aware that his mind can see things his hands can't draw yet. Because minds grow faster than hands, we have to wait for the hands to catch up. Meanwhile, practice can increase fine motor control, and a child-controlled program of practice is a good first step toward dealing with giftedness.

Until the motor skills catch up, sometimes reversing the scale removes the imbalance. When one preschooler was frustrated to tears because she couldn't draw small enough to fit everything she wanted to show on a piece of paper, her mom took her outside where they turned the patio into a chalk mural with a cast of dozens, all easily drawn in scale befitting

Mount Rushmore. The mural in this story lasted until the first rain; the moral, much longer.

INTROVERSION

Personality type is a major factor in self-concept. One very common trait is introversion. According to Linda Silverman of Denver University and the Gifted Child Development Center there, extroverts comprise seventy-five percent of the population in American society, but introverts make up as much as sixty percent of the gifted population.

If your child is among that majority-within-a-minority, that information may help the "goodness-of-fit" you share. For example, it could help you tolerate your preschooler's need to observe before trying a new activity, or her need to think before sharing ideas, and the need to have time alone. Self-acceptance comes in large part from being accepted by those close to one, and it is essential to a healthy self-concept.

Silverman has compiled a list of the characteristics of introverts:

- Needs time alone.
- Needs time to observe before trying new activities.
- Becomes embarrassed or humiliated easily in public.
- Thinks through ideas before sharing them with others.
- Has intense need for privacy.
- Desires one best friend, rather than many friends.
- May try to be "perfect" in public, then vent negative feelings and frustrations at home.
- Likes to concentrate on one activity at a time.
- Hates being interrupted.
- May appear very different in public than in private.
- Can mask feelings.
- Is slow to respond to people and situations, needing time to think.
- Is more aware of his/her own thoughts than of others'.
- Rarely talks about his/her feelings or problems.
- May feel lonely even if others want to be with him/her.
- May prefer to read rather than be with others.

Just reading that list can be an eye-opener for parents. An introverted third-grader whose parents showed her that list was fascinated to find that she felt every one of those descriptions matched her personality. This knowledge can help parents and teachers learn to accept behavior that can sometimes be frustrating and even mistaken for below-average performance. Performance could be skewed by the tension inherent in the do-or-die tests.

A study of self-concept by Paul Janos, Helen Fung, and Nancy Robinson conducted at the Child Development Research Group at the University of Washington found that high-IQ children *who perceive themselves as different* had significantly lower self-concept scores than gifted children who didn't see themselves as different. "Children may experience a need to minimize differences from peers, but lack methods for constructively doing so. . . . An enlightened adult can provide support in managing the problem. They need help in gaining a balanced view of their own self-worth in a social as well as intellectual context."

To minimize the feeling that he is exceptional:

- Try looking for activities that your child may enjoy with his age peers: playground, parks, bikes, ball games, and other activities that rely on chance rather than thinking skills.
- Help them see that we all play many roles in our livges; and that each person brings his own talents and skills to the mix, and we're all richer for the diversity.
- Compliment your child and her companions for their positive actions in social as well as intellectual or skill areas. Too much attention to their attributes leads to frustration; some children feel they're loved for their abilities, not themselves, and fear that if they perform below their ability the love is not earned, and therefore may be withdrawn.
- Praise your child, too, for the effort and persistence he puts forth and the ingenuity his creation shows—not just for the end product.
- Be aware of the problems that may come hand in hand with exceptional talents or skills. As comedian George Carlin has said, "Behind every silver lining . . . there's a dark cloud."

A teacher and counselor of gifted children, Nancy Johnson, has written about the both "a blessing and a curse" view of some of the attributes and behavior of gifted children, citing some of the ways those same qualities might be considered liabilities by other people. Just as the glass that the optimist sees as half- full but is called half-empty by the pessimist, the same behavior might mean different things to people who see them from different perspectives. For example:

You find little Billy refreshingly candid, frank, and informal. His teacher may feel he has a big mouth.

Lisa's kindergarten teacher loved her quick mastery of new material, but her first-grade teacher wishes she would repeat and drill with the rest of the class.

Tim's art teacher appreciates his unwavering persistence; his gym teacher finds him stubborn.

Rachel's nursery school teacher appreciates her ability to concentrate intensely, but at the same time wishes she could drop one activity and turn to another on schedule.

You might find Brett wonderfully receptive and open to any new thought; some of his street-smart buddies consider him gullible.

Alissa is called sensitive, intuitive, and empathetic, but at the same time she seems overly sensitive to criticism and vulnerable to peer rejection.

Paul's teacher praises his self-reliant, independent nature, but can't fit him into a study group for a cooperative team project.

Halfway through reading class, David has finished his week's story and the next two in the reader. His teacher tells you he can never find his place when asked to read the next paragraph.

Tina sings so well that the teacher asks her to lead the class singing. Her classmates complain that she consistently pitches songs beyond their range.

If having a gifted child seems like holding a bag of gold coins, remember that every coin has two sides. Discovering that your child is gifted doesn't mean your problems are over and you can lean back, put your feet up, and coast. You still have problems; they are simply of a different type and magnitude, but most can be solved with loving, patient, calm, and creative attention.

SOCIAL DEVELOPMENT

While taking stock of your child's development, it's essential to take a good look at his overall social and moral growth. The development that began with the emergence of self-concept in the toddler stage is continuing, and with it the child's position in relation to those around him.

As we discussed earlier, it is important that the preschooler accept responsibility for his actions or nonactions. Empathy, sensitivity to others' feelings, sharing, and taking turns are cornerstones of this foundation.

Long before we place the child in school, it's important to look ahead and think about what kind of child we want to send. How will he function there? Which of his attributes are we encouraging, and what will be their impact on his school experience?

One of the trailblazers in the field of gifted children is Paul Torrance. The first chapter of his *Gifted Children in the Classroom* deserves posting in teachers' lounges, because it could help more teachers understand some of the aspects of giftedness. After all, just as parents recognize that raising a gifted child takes more specialized guidance than others, so do teachers know that a handful of them in a classroom can add whirlpools and backwashes to waters that would otherwise flow smoothly.

Naturally, many teachers welcome all the gifted students they can add to the mix; they thrive on the challenge and the dynamics they bring. Others, however, are more threatened than challenged; they prefer the smooth sailing that sometimes comes from homogeneity.

Torrance contrasts for us the ten characteristics most prized in students by American teachers with those rated by a panel of experts to be essential to a productive, creative person. It's easy to conclude that not every teacher would love a third of each class to be gifted.

For example, the teachers' dream student, reasonably enough, would be considerate of others; an independent thinker; determined; industrious; posssessing a sense of humor; curious; sincere; courteous; timely in finishing work; and healthy.

The educators empaneled to nominate the productive, creative students' attributes picked only two of those qualities, curiosity and independent thinking. The others were intellectual courage or courage of one's convictions; independence in judgment; becoming absorbed and preoccupied with tasks; intuitiveness; persistence; unwillingness to accept ideas on mere say-so; willingness to take risks; unwillingness to accept unquestioningly the judgments of authorities.

It's worth noting some of Torrance's insights about the teachers' wishlist as those attributes apply to gifted students.

Regarding consideration for others, Torrance suggests that placing consideration at the top of a hierarchy of values may reflect an overemphasis on conformity to the thinking of others, which could work against the freeing of potentiality or indicate a subtle conditioning for dishonesty.

On determination: "Perhaps teachers and parents need to teach some determined, creatively gifted children how to give in occasionally without giving up."

Regarding the appearance of industriousness: highly creative people may not appear industrious because they are not *visibly* busy; giving thinking a status of legitimacy might deemphasize "appearing to be" busy, which is an acquired trait of underlying dishonesty.

As for promptness on deadlines: "The tyranny of the clock is a mighty enemy of imaginative thinking."

On sense of humor: Some gifted children take on the cloak of class clown to deflect attention from their differentness. For others it can be a defensive weapon, using satire or sarcasm to bludgeon without bruising. The teacher and parent can help channel the use of humor in the creative pupil to avoid letting it become obnoxious, hostile, or excessively silly.

Finally, sincerity: "Parents and teachers pay lip service to the importance of sincerity and honesty, yet subtly condition children in many ways to be dishonest. Both parents and teachers should be careful to pay more than lip service when the sincere thoughts and feelings expressed by children are not all the clean and holy ones that we approve or are different from ours."

Whatever attributes are on your list, it helps to stop from time to time to assess what kind of person you want your child to become. As his abilities grow and his self-concept develops alongside, it's important to have the right balance of respect and admiration between parent and child. Feelings are easily hurt, and we tend to forget that a gifted child's emotional development is often at or below chronological age level, especially when language and behavior are like those of much older children.

A successful parent-child relationship must allow for growth and adaptation. Parents need to support (even when they do not agree with or allow) a gifted child's assertiveness by enabling the child to make some choices, such as which clothes to wear. But even gifted children need to be assessed to make sure they do their share of household tasks—otherwise they'll evade them for the rest of their lives. Instead of fighting their brightness, use it on your behalf by including the child in defining limits and dividing up tasks.

One mother of two gifted preschoolers helped them learn to enforce schedules on their own with a kitchen timer. When one became interested in practicing music, they used it to time how long she would play. The mother would read at night for a preannounced duration; when the bell rang to signal quitting time, the girls didn't protest or beg to prolong. They accepted the neutral role of the mechanical signal: "When it rang," their mother recalls, "they knew it was time to finish up, and then I'd tell them good night."

A positive and patient sense of home as a learning environment, of home as a child's garden for growing, helps build a self-image that is not limited by age or body size. Pets help, too, by teaching children about responsibility and reverence for life. They can teach caring and unselfish love.

Religion can help the child find an independent sense of identity with a sense of security and love. This can be communicated through saying prayers or hymns with the child in the morning and evening, as many parents have told us they do. The so-called Golden Rule, found in different forms in many religions, is a concept that can provide the solid basis for communicating effective behavior to the gifted child who wants to know the "why" behind regulations.

Here are some suggestions and observations on supporting the self-concept and moral development of 3- and 4-year-old gifted children, as garnered from parents:

- Keep rules few and clear.
- Remember that you're on your child's side; take actions that encourage independence. Buy clothes, for example, with simple closures so that he can dress himself; then leave a choice of clothing so he can pick an ensemble you can live with.
- Don't overschedule; allow time for imagination or creativity; let your child know his thoughts are private and safe.
- Remember the importance of play and games in moral development; use dramatic play—puppets, role-playing—to challenge thinking on moral issues, allowing the child to provide his own solutions; appreciate humor as a talent worth developing; watch for growth in your child's reasoning ability over time.
- Allow customs, motifs, and personal styles to develop; build on them.

- Instead of merely correcting, repeat and embellish what your child says.
- Talk about feelings, using dolls or toys where helpful, to allow him to express himself; use "mirroring" to reflect or echo his emotions.
- If possible, don't interrupt a little one who's absorbed in a project, observation, or fantasy.
- Encourage questions and respectful challenges, goal setting and skill mastery by the child, without applying pressure.

One parent used these rules for her older preschoolers:

1. No toys left on the main floor by bedtime.
2. Clothes and linens would be laundered *if put in the hamper.*
3. While she would "assist" when invited, each child was responsible for straightening his own room.

Encouraging a child's whole sense of self through high self-esteem, self-confidence, and moral values, with the special mix of love and discipline that marks an aware parent, is a gift more valuable than tennis lessons, coordinated sheets and curtains, or a personal stereo.

ACTIVITIES

Without enrolling in a university lab school, taking correspondence courses in preschool methods, or investing a great deal of money in equipment, there are a number of things you can do in and near your home to sharpen your preschooler's skills and augment areas where you feel he may need extra help.

Math

Our goal is not to present an encyclopedic list, but rather suggest the kinds of things that will in turn suggest others. These will be appropriate at different ages for different preschoolers, so test and go with what works. Our suggestions are meant to be evocative springboards; the ones you dream up will be better for your child and situation. "Give a man a fish and he has food for one day, but teach a man to fish and he has food for life," goes the adage. Or, as a teacher of gifted children has said, "I always wonder when I see seminars of '101 activities to do with your gifted child': What do you do on Day 102?"

Start with math. Your first goal might be to help your child build his math perception and vocabulary:

- Spatial: up, down, outside, inside, top, bottom, above, below, beside.
- Descriptive: open, closed, round, straight, sharp, point, corner, flat, smooth, bumpy.
- Quantitative: how many, more, less, fewer, same number, numeral names.
- Comparisons: big/little, long/short, tall/short, high/low, wide/narrow, heavy/light, dark/light, loud/quiet, hard/soft, bigger than, smaller than, more than, less than, same as, largest, smallest.

Use these concepts in your daily life; point out usage in your conversations; ask your child to notice, describe, and contribute. Talk about shapes; find them and identify them in objects or pictures in and around your home. Conduct a triangle hunt on your walk around the block. Find shapes in books you're reading. Walk through the basement and visualize what room or furnishings are above you. Draw a plan view of a room, your house, or your block as it would appear to a fly on the ceiling or a bird in a tree or you if you could float overhead in a balloon. (If your child doesn't respond to mapmaking yet, put this one on hold for a few months and trot it out later.)

Next, allow the child to use counting and simple problem-solving and sorting exercises as part of your daily routine. Putting away the clean silverware teaches sorting and classifying. Setting the table involves simple equations: Normally there are six of us; today your brother is at the library but your Aunt Ann is here with your cousin Jessica. How many places will we set? Will you help me sort this laundry? Let's put all socks in this pile, and then gather them in pairs. We're baking a cake today; will you help me measure the ingredients? Here are six cookies. Give the same number to your brother, sister, and yourself. How old are your sister and brother, and how old will they be on their next birthday? How many years older (younger) is your sister? When you are 8, how old will she be? When she is 10, how old will you be? (Stay with this program only as long as it's working; back off when it gets frustrating.)

Then provide math-oriented toys: beads, spools, buttons to sort and count; Cuisenaire rods; dominoes; parquetry blocks; a felt board with various colors, shapes, and sizes; balance scales; measuring cups and a dishpan for measuring beans, sand, pebbles, rice, or water. Play bingo. Use board games with dice and markers that move along a course of squares.

Next try some simple add-and-subtract exercises with payoffs they can sink their teeth into: use peanuts, M & Ms, or fruit pieces. Groups of things that look alike are called *sets*. Here are two sets of peanuts (four and six in two groups). How can we make both sets the same?

Give your child tape measure, ruler, and yardstick; allow her to measure things around the house. Think about which device is appropriate to use on different objects.

Give the child his own calendar. (Bookstores close them out some time after New Year's; look for the large-format ones with illustrations from children's books. Later on these can be covered with clear plastic and displayed.) Let him write or draw special events like picnics, birthdays, or adventures in the daily squares. Ask him to depict the weather conditions with sun, cloud, raindrop, snowman, or anything he chooses. Count the days as they progress through the month and the months through the year. Conduct countdowns to important days—birthdays, visits, special events.

Finance some purchase at the store; let your child pay the cashier and take the change. Show the coins and denominations; arrange them at home in sets; show various configurations of a dollar. Use Monopoly game money to walk through the purchase of a gallon of ice cream, a bicycle, a new car. (Some toy stores now sell bundles of the money separately.)

Introduce relative time concepts. (Your sister will be home when school gets out at 3:30—that's an hour from now, when "Sesame Street" is over. The cookies will be done in seven minutes; I'll set the timer to ring then.)

Encourage the child to estimate and check the accuracy of the estimate. How many cookies are in this jar? How long will it take to drive to the store?

Libraries and bookstores will provide more ideas and materials. The Missouri New Parents as Teachers project has a booklet, "Exploring Math Experiences"; *Preparing Young Children for Math* by Claudia Zaslavsky is another very useful source.

Science

Listen to weather reports and forecasts and watch for cloud conditions to presage changes. Use an outdoor thermometer to report air temperature; set up comfort guidelines that depend on the outside temperature; let your child help set the guidelines and notice when he's hot or cold. Look at animals and plants as they react to weather and changing seasons. See where the snow melts first and last, and where water pools after rain. Watch for a rainbow, then use a prism to make a spectrum of light. Mark shadows to measure the earth's rotation in one hour. Take periodic walks and choose flowering shrubs or trees to watch from year to year. Hunt for buds, seeds, nests and eggs, insects, falling leaves, cocoons. Notice the territorial calls of nesting birds—cardinals and redwing blackbirds, for example. Imitate their calls if you're a proficient whistler; some will carry on quite a call-and-response dialogue with you. Draw a map of your route; keep a journal (which originally meant a log of a day's trip, a diary of a journey).

Do some simple experiments. Watch an ice cube melt on a sunny sidewalk. Put another cube alongside and sprinkle salt on it. Place several objects in a pan of water. Which ones float and which sink?

Your child can plant seeds in potting soil, and water and care for them. Find and identify the seeds on plants and trees and within fruits and vegetables. Use egg cartons if bedding pots aren't handy. Try some experiments; plant seeds and deprive water and light from half of them.

Learn to set up classifying exercises: fruits and vegetables; living and inanimate objects; mammals versus reptiles; things you can smell; others you can't see but can hear.

Develop awareness of all senses as part of the joy of discovery: show her several objects on the table—eyeglasses, key ring, flower, paper clip, shoelace, plastic bandage—then cover them and ask her to name as many as she can recall. Show them again; cover her eyes; remove one; ask her to look over the array and identify the missing item. Cover her eyes again and ask her to describe what you're doing from the sound alone—shut a door, draw a shade, pour water, drop pennies in a bottle, cut paper, blow up a balloon, close a zipper, open a can of carbonated beverage, or whatever comes to mind. Open jars of spices; let her sniff and try to name them. When you simmer a pot roast, add a little of everything into the broth: cola, lemon juice, Tabasco sauce, orange juice, horseradish—then while you're eating, see who can identify the most ingredients. When you're driving home, wait till the child recognizes your neighborhood, then ask her to close her eyes and tell you when she perceives you are near your own driveway.

Outfit him with a prism, magnifying glass and insect jar, and magnets. Turn him loose to discover what he can.

Try to encourage investigation; ask leading questions without providing the answers; and allow synthesis from one field to another. Remember that all children benefit from picking up facts. Some children are more likely to cross-pollinate from disparate fields, form their own conclusions, invent new applications, and apply findings from one area to unknowns in another; it is these synthesizers that we call gifted children.

Cross-pollinate on your own. Combine a visit to the zoo with a trip to the library to discover more about endangered species, or a favorite family of animals. When you rout a raccoon from your attic, follow through with trips to the forest preserve or wildlife reservation. See how animals adapt to changing environments and food supplies. If you don't have all the wildlife programs from public television on videocassette, rent one from the library or video rental when a question becomes meaningful to the child: they are eloquent and memorable depictions of animal behavior and places too remote for any of us to visit.

Art

Begin by surrounding your child with a visually enriched atmosphere—not noisy and distracting, but stimulating and interesting with a constantly evolving variety of materials. Provide supplies: old magazines to tear or cut apart; markers, chalk, scissors, glue, paint, clay, and collage materials. For a good head start in organizing a home work space and materials, find *Doing Art Together*, by Muriel Silberstein-Storfer with Mablen Jones.

Have places to save and display your child's art. One family rigged a family room gallery with wooden frames in which current artwork is displayed; it's an unjuried show that changes constantly. Keep finished pieces in a portfolio; hold a backyard clothesline art show for family, friends and neighbors.

Make specific positive comments about the use of color, balance, composition, use of space, texture, and contrasts, for example. Avoid the general "That's a nice picture." Encourage imaginative use of media or techniques; until we "teach" it out of them, some kids come to the table with limitless creativity. When colors run together, ask them to describe the process. Don't ask "What is it?"; a better approach is "Tell me about it."

Now introduce some examples to stretch the mind. Visit art museums just to wander, not to preach. Let them go where they wish; point out contrasts or ask questions that encourage evaluation of what they're seeing. At the museum store, buy a dozen or more postcards, especially of pieces you remember seeing on your walk. Get as many widely disparate examples as you can. Display them all in a group and compare and contrast them. Try to guess why the artist used the color or composition or viewpoint that he did. Rent or borrow a piece from the museum or a library. (Many libraries circulate museum prints; change them every few weeks and make sure every style and period are represented. Compare and contrast again.)

Children's books are better illustrated every year. Once the mortar between the bricks, or perhaps frosting on the cake, illustration has become as important as the text of children's literature, and we are much better off as a result. As you read, talk about different styles. You may find that the child begins to recognize an artist's work from the style of the cover before he can read the title and name.

Read together Leo Lionni's *Little Blue and Little Yellow* and the many books of photographs of Tana Hoban that concentrate on color, shapes, and spatial concepts: *Is It Red? Is It Yellow? Is It Blue?*; *26 Letters and 99 Cents*; *Red, Blue, Yellow Shoe*; and *Shapes, Shapes, Shapes*.

Music

Once again, variety is essential to good balance. Let your child hear music from the radio, records and tapes, and instruments you own or to which you have access. (Remember that silence is eloquent; nonstop sound may be hard to discern.)

Introduce melody and rhythm through familiar tunes—nursery rhymes, children's records, folk songs, lullabies, or rope-jumping songs. Then equip your child with pan-lid cymbals, rhythm sticks (which can be two lengths of hardwood dowel), sandpaper blocks, tambourine, oatmeal boxes with wooden spoons, and measuring cups. Now sing and move and clang along with your favorite music.

It's important to allow creativity as your child moves; different selections may inspire different movements. Establish the rhythm with drum or sticks, encouraging the child to match the tempo you're beating. Then move to simple melodies with clear and consistent rhythms. Don't overdirect; allow freedom to choose movements that seem appropriate.

Social Studies

Make a map of your immediate neighborhood, marking places familiar to your child; talk about the scale and symbols you use. Look at a printed map of your community; help her orient herself to landmarks she recognizes.

Let your child formulate a list of community services your family needs to support its existence: Who would help if we had a fire? A burglary? A large hole in the roadway? An injury? A death? An epidemic?

Talk about elections; let your child see you vote; discuss what voting means in a family meeting that deals with the issues. Vote on dessert or a menu for a future dinner.

Find puzzles of the United States and of the world. Work on them informally with your child. Show him where he lives; where relatives live, where Paddington Bear came from (Darkest Peru); if possible, get a globe.

Discuss your family's cultural and national heritage. Trace the movement of previous generations; touch on what the world was like in those times and the motivation for emigration.

Let your child plan, cook, and eat a meal from a different culture.

Find and learn a dance, myth, costume, story, and/or song from another culture or country of origin of an ancestor. Visit a church from another faith. Research and commemorate a holiday from a different faith. Compare and contrast with holidays in your own tradition.

When your child becomes interested, take a field trip to study Native Americans; learn what tribes and nations populated the region you now occupy. (An excellent resource for this is Carl Waldman's *Atlas of the North American Indian*.) Research what life was like for children of that tribe. Replicate clothing that might have been worn by them.

Retreat to a forest or undeveloped area and imagine what it must have looked like a century ago. Visit the oldest cemetary in the region; read the names on the markers to see if any are still familiar; use the dates to calculate the ages.

Read beginner biographies of famous people—*Abraham Lincoln* by d'Aulaire, Alike's *A Weed Is a Flower*, or *Johnny Appleseed*. Read simple fairy tales, folktales, myths, and legends.

Visit a local nursing home; try to meet a long-time resident with good recall of what your area was like in his/her childhood.

As we mentioned, these are idea starters. Adapt any that seem interesting at the time they also seem to inspire motivation in your child. But don't push. If the ideas don't click, put them aside until later.

Language Development

If a child is potentially gifted, language is the road map to the world within the person; it is the framework of thought, the currency of discourse; it is the shortest distance to some things the child wants; it is the lens through which perceptions are focused; it is the foundation of understanding; it is the earliest measurable empirical evidence of intelligence; and it is the easiest testing indicator.

On our way to treating all the other things language is, we'll begin with this last, the testing indicator. Louis Terman's early study of gifted children in 1924 identified language as a reliable index of high intelligence. What can a parent do to stimulate rich language in his children?

TALK TO YOUR CHILD

Five techniques are set down by Joyce Ury Dumtschin in the journal of the National Association for the Education of Young Children, *Young Children*. They are:

- Modeling—using appropriate language correctly and imaginatively. The child draws from words and usages he or she hears.
- Expatiation—elaborating, adding relevant information to the topic the child has introduced.
- Open-ended questioning—asking a question that calls for a divergent answer rather than one word.

- Expansion—corrected feedback partially restating a child's incomplete statement to make it complete, without a negative response or insisting on a correction.
- Recasting—replaying a child's statement, preserving the content but altering the grammatical structure.

Perhaps the most beneficial of these is the open-ended question. Too often teachers and parents fall into a rut of asking "known-answer" questions, which require almost no processing; sometimes even a shrug or gesture would be as good as the called-for word.

The best preschool teachers, consciously or not, are frequently the ones who rely least on known-answer questions. They keep the kids on their toes, and new connections are constantly being made. Rita Haynes Blocksom, a school consultant, in an article in *Preschool Perspectives* (February 1987) offers some sample open-ended questions:

- What would happen if dogs were as big as houses?
- How many ways can you rock when you're sitting down?
- What would you do if you got lost?
- What else could you do with a sock if you couldn't wear it?
- What would happen if you had eyes in the back of your head?
- How would the story of Snow White be different if the dwarfs were big and Snow White were little?

PLAY WITH WORDS

Keep the air in your house full of interesting words. Just as you catch more flies with honey than with vinegar, you elicit a lot more interest and involvement if the words you use are just plain fun.

Because the youngest children first learn to identify the first and last sounds in words, start with rhyme and alliterations. Make up sentences with as many rhymes or same initial sounds as possible. One gifted 3-year-old and her mom came up with "Kate the great wrote on her slate to her mate Nate who was late for their date: I'd better go now to milk the cow, but I don't know how so join me now." Buy Betty's Better, Not-too-Bitter Butter Batter. (They barter? You betcha.) Be word collectors. Install a chalkboard in the kitchen and use it often as a visible record of your conversations. Make it large enough for your writing at the top to be out of the eraser's reach but low enough for her to have room to copy when she becomes ready to try writing.

When the time is right, introduce puns. Make up jokes using them, nonsense songs, silly sayings, new verses to familiar tunes. Notice words on your travels—read signs, read to your child the backs of cereal boxes, the aisle markers in the grocery store, store names, stop signs, logos on television commercials. Play the alphabet game when you're driving—find the letter A on signs, then find a B in turn, then a C.

When you run out of ideas, it's probably time to try a book.

READ CHILDREN'S BOOKS

There are more fine, imaginative, evocative children's books today than ever. The last decade has seen a renaissance in the field. There are even books that guide you to the best of those books.

It's not always possible to say that a given book is good for a certain age level. Children develop at widely varied rates, of course, and gifted children are generally ready for more variety and more sophisticated material before their peers. Besides, many books are written to be appreciated at many levels and so bear rereading from time to time.

There is enormous variety in store for you and your child—in fairy tales, nursery rhymes and tales, old and modern classics, poetry, and lots of wonderful artwork. Illustration has become more sophisticated, with a wide range of media to expand the imagination.

If you're not already a regular at your local library, now's your chance. Let your child come to anticipate regular visits. Try to allow enough time so he can browse and explore. Take armloads of books home and wallow in them for a week or two, then visit again for some new ones and some old favorites.

At your local bookstore, you may have to hunt a little for good books that aren't yet best-sellers. If you're fortunate enough to have a well-stocked children's book department nearby, patronize it and tell your friends. One publisher worth mentioning is Picture Book Studio. Some of the most beautifully produced books in recent years have been the loving product of this firm. They secure rights to publish some of the finest new European children's literature and some retellings of classic stories beautifully illustrated by such artists as Lisbeth Zwerger and

Chihiro Iwasaki. Some of Eric Carle's books are on their list; his imaginative use of format in books like *Papa, Please Get the Moon for Me* captivates both children and adults. If your local library and bookstores don't have them, you can order direct from the publisher, Picture Book Studio USA, 60 North Main St., Natick, MA 01760.

In our haste to be the first by whom the new is tried, let's be slow to lay the old aside. Some wonderful books for children were written and illustrated in time to be read to us by our parents; nothing is quite like holding your children in your lap and reading them something your mother or father read to you. The following books are still in circulation: *Mother Goose, Goodnight Moon* (Margaret Wise Brown), *The Story of Ferdinand* (Munro Leaf), *The Biggest Bear* (Lynd Ward), *The Little House* and *Mike Mulligan and His Steam Shovel* (Virginia Burton), *Blueberries for Sal* and *Make Way for Ducklings* (Robert McCloskey), *Curious George* (H. A. Rey), *Play With Me* (Marie Hall Ets), *Madeleine* (Ludwig Bemelmans), *Babar* (Jean deBrunhoff), *The Country Bunny and the Little Gold Shoes* (duBose Heyward), and *Wait for William* (Marjorie Flack).

Moreover, there are lots of cross-cultural adventures waiting. Folk tales can be good springboards for discussions of other cultures. Tomie de Paola, who has done a couple of dozen books, none of which you'd want to part with, tells the Italian tale of *Strega Nona*. The Japanese story of *The Funny Little Women* was set by Arlene Mosel. Verna Aardema retells *Why Mosquitoes Buzz in People's Ears*, an African tale. Ruth Sawyer captured the American folk tale of *Journey Cake Ho*. Among treatments of fables we recommend for preschoolers are Eric Carle's *Twelve Tales from Aesop* and Arnold Lobel's *Fables*.

Don't neglect good monochrome illustration in favor of full-color books, by the way. Dorothy Butler in *Babies Need Books* writes,

> as experience widens, and the taste refines, the graphic quality of a picture is tempered by other considerations. Sensitivity to line and form and a feeling for relationship develop unconsciously through access to the best picture books, but are unlikely to emerge spontaneously in the youngster whose experience of books has been limited. . . . The bright lights and loud noises (even excluding the effects of television) have a lot to answer for in the impairment of the child's sense of wonder.

Millions of Cats by Wanda Gag, *In the Forest* by Marie Hall Ets, and Judith Viorst's *Sunday Morning* are all richly illustrated in monochrome.

Poetry is the highest form of verbal art. Poets paint with words. You can say things in a poem that just wouldn't come across right in prose.

A. A. Milne's *When We Were Very Young* and *Now We Are Six* are excellent first books of poetry, richly loaded with situations young children indentify with. Edward Lear's *The Owl and the Pussycat*, Beatrice Schenk DeRegniers' *May I Bring a Friend*, and works by Jack Prelutsky and Aileen Fisher are each worth a library visit.

And then there's Shel Silverstein, who doesn't quite fit on any list, except of best-selling authors. He first gained celebrity as a singer-songwriter and illustrator, but his visibility among younger readers increased when he wrote *The Giving Tree* and Peter, Paul and Mary sang his "I'm Being Eaten by a Boa Constrictor" on their children's album, "Peter, Paul, and Mommy." Two collections of his poems published by Harper and Row, *Where the Sidewalk Ends* and *The Light in the Attic*, are about as far removed from fields of waving daffodils as any collection of poems could be. Today's hippest pre-teens can dig poetry without losing cool with stuff like this around. With judicious selection they are fun for younger kids, but some might be a little earthy to be read by impressionable parents.

As you and your child read together you will find a number of favorites. We have always followed FitzHugh Dodson's advice to identify the author and illustrator of every book to the child, for two reasons. First, the child understands from the beginning that someone, somewhere, created this book after personal effort; by extension, so might your child, one day. Second, as you read more works, the styles of certain authors or illustrators or both will become favorites; identify them when that happens. Remind him of the other books by this person that the two of you have read together. This encourages the child to identify similarities and to assimilate elements of style—the first steps toward evaluating and developing favorite artists.

You might have to do some browsing in your library. Some picture books may be found among the folk tales, for example.

In any event, consider books by these authors and/or illustrators worth looking into with your child: Martha Alexander, Aliki, Mitsumasa Anno, Lorna Balian, Judi Barrett, Marcia Brown, John Burningham, Barbara Cooney, Tomie dePaola, William Pene duBois, Ivan Gantschev, Lillian and Russell Hoban, Tana Hoban, Nanny Hogrogian, Ezra Jack Keats, Steven Kellogg, Jean Lexau, Leo Lionni, Arnold Lobel, Mercer Mayer, Bill Peet, Maurice Sendak, Peter Spier, William Steig, Chris Van Allsberg, Brian Wildsmith, Taro Yashima, Charlotte Zolotow.

This is just a beginning; there are many more. See other ideas in our sources of children's books.

Books are springboards for launching creative thoughts and thinking skills. One story leads to another. From this leapfrogging comes the ability to synthesize, a basic thinking skill.

Here are a few things you can do to keep a book alive and push the margins of your child's awareness:

- Make finger or hand puppets to act out the story or to create your own sequels.
- Use craft materials to construct characters or settings from the story.
- Make "thumbprint" pictures of the characters with a stamp pad and your fingers, and a pencil.
- Illustrate the story with finger paints or a chalkboard.
- Act out episodes from the story in impromptu performance.
- Read related stories or collateral information about some element of the story—reference, history, or the natural features of a region.
- Imagine being in the thick of the action; what would your child do? How would she dress?
- Apply a lesson or moral from the story to other situations.
- Make up an original game based on the story's plot.
- Draw a map of the main setting of the story.

Here are some reliable books, mostly for teachers but also adaptable for home use, suggesting further activities that tie into specific books:

- *Books in Bloom: Developing Creativity Through Literature*, by Connie Champlin and Barbara Kennedy. Special Literature Press, Omaha, NE, 1982. Applies Bloom's taxonomy (Knowledge, Application, Analysis, Synthesis, and Evaluation) to children's literature, demonstrated by activities specific to the recommended books, including *The Amazing Bone, Ben's Trumpet, Crow Boy, The Girl Who Loved Horses, The Ice Cream Cone Coot, The Mystery of the Missing Red Mitten, Owliver, Ox-Cart Man, The Search for Delicious, Strega Nona, The Sweet Touch, The Taily Po, Why Mosquitoes Buzz in People's Ears,* and *The Wishing Hat.*
- *E is for everybody: A manual for bringing fine picture books into the hands and hearts of children*, by Nancy Polette. Scarecrow Press, Metuchen, NJ, 1976. Lists 147 picture books with brief summaries and ideas for

activities for primary and intermediate students; many are adaptable for preschoolers.

- *Books and Real Life: A Guide for Gifted Students and Teachers*, by Nancy Polette. McFarland & Co., Jefferson, NC, 1984. Realistic fiction for preschool through intermediate children. Plot summaries and sample questions to promote thinking and discussion. Polette claims:
- The field of literature for children and young adults abounds with excellent realistic fiction which can serve as a springboard to real-life, problem-solving experiences.
- Every good story is a problem-solving experience. The nature of any story is conflict. As children examine the many ways in which a protagonist deals with conflict they begin to examine values and make judgments and decisions for their own lives.
- *Picture Books for Gifted Programs*, by Nancy Polette. Scarecrow Press, Metuchen, NJ, 1981. Cites picture books that encourage development of specific concepts: conservation (the ability to recognize shapes such as letters in various forms), classification (the ability to classify objects and ideas), seriation (placing objects or events in order), and reversibility (tracing reasoning backward; essential in appreciating humor or satire, literal *and* implied meaning). Also identifies:

> More than three dozen books that promote visual literacy
> More than two dozen that stimulate language development
> A dozen that challenge productive thinking (fluency and flexibility, originality, elaboration, and evaluation)
> Three dozen more to foster critical thinking (planning, forecasting, decision making, problem solving)

Other sources of good books to read:

- *The Reading Out Loud Handbook*, Jim Trelease. One day newspaper writer-illustrator Trelease, parent of two, turned off the television. His children cried for four months. After that they grew up listening and reading, and are much enriched for the experience. This work tells you what's good about more than three hundred books you might want to read with your children—and cross-references others of similar bent in case you hit the jackpot and want to extend the winning streak.

- *Children and Books*, by Zena Sutherland, Diane L. Monson, and May Hill Arbuthnot.
- *The Book Finder: When Children Need Books* by Sharon Spredemann Dreyer. The operative word here is "need." The author offers more than one thousand listings, summarized and cross-referenced by topics and emotions treated in the stories. Thus it's an excellent reference for bibliotherapy, the modeling of solutions to readers' problems.
- *Best Books for Children: Preschool through the Middle Grades*. Edited by John T. Gillespie and Christine B. Gilbert; New York: R. R. Bowker Company, third edition in 1985. Publisher's information, price, age level, and brief descriptions of over nine thousand books in the first 422 pages; then 175 pages of cross-indexes. Primarily a librarian's reference book but handy for tracking down a book you half-remember or for prospecting a category your child has just discovered.
- *The New York Times Parent's Guide to the Best Books for Children*, by Eden Ross Lipson, Times Books, 1988, lists 956 books from Wordless Picture Books to Young Adult Books, and indexes them in thirty-four different groups—by title, illustrator, age-appropriateness, read-aloud affinity, and more than a dozen category/subject listings. Who could be more on top of current offerings in children's books than the *Times'* full-time reviewer?
- *Guiding Gifted Readers from Preschool through High School: A Handbook for Parents, Teachers, Counselors and Librarians*, by Judith Wynn Halsted, Ohio Psychology Publishing Co., 1988. This book is a comprehensive guide on using books to promote the emotional and intellectual development of the gifted child. Halsted describes how thoughtfully chosen books can help gifted children develop a healthy identity, learn to get along with others, and use their abilities. She explains how bibliotherapy, the use of books for help in solving personal problems, can be employed "to help gifted youngsters recognize and articulate their feelings, and to prepare them for the particular spins that being gifted puts on the normal developmental tasks faced by all children."

Halsted discusses the typical reading patterns of children at various age levels and the need for gentle guidance to steer children to books that will fulfill both their emotional and intellectual needs. She states, for example, that

Fiction will fall naturally into the hands of gifted elementary school children, but unless a planned effort is made to introduce young readers to other branches of literature, especially traditional literature and poetry, they may miss them altogether.

Guiding Gifted Readers includes an annotated bibliography divided into five age groups: Preschool-Kindergarten, Early Elementary (Grades 1-3), Upper Elementary (Grades 4-5), Junior High (7-9), and Senior High (10-12). Within each age grouping, books are listed under five categories:

- Identity (which includes books that can be used to encourage the development of a strong self-concept and acceptance of giftedness as a positive part of one's identity)
- Aloneness (including books that help gifted children to explore the positive aspects of time spent alone)
- Getting Along with Others (with books that facilitate discussion of friendship, interdependence, empathy, and respect for others with lesser or different abilities)
- Developing Imagination (for younger children through early elementary—includes books to stimulate thinking, observing, and questioning). Or Using Abilities (for older children—which describes books dealing with decision making and the responsibilities and rewards of special talents)
- Drive to Understand (with books to challenge children intellectually)

These are just a beginning; many others are at your library. As with children's books, you may have to search a bit before you find the books that are best for you.

If your 3½ or 4-year-old has a long attention span, try reading from some of the longer books with chapters. Milne's *Winnie the Pooh* and *House at Pooh Corner* and E. B. White's *Charlotte's Web* are usually good starting points. But remember that some styles just don't connect with some children. One mother could never interest her kindergartner in any animal fantasies, although her brother had loved *Wind in the Willows* at 4 and a sister thrived on Beatrix Potter's Peter Rabbit books at 2. One night the girl was afflicted with chicken pox, standing in the need of distraction. Her mother tried Beverly Cleary's *Ramona the Pest*; that one worked. They read the first four or five in the series that week.

When you're reading aloud, don't be afraid to edit long background passages or elaborate descriptions. Sometimes it helps tailor a book meant for much older readers for a child who's ready for the plot and concept. Good books are meant to be read and reread and appreciated on different levels. Chapter breaks are good excuses to allow the child to control your traversal; it's an excuse to stop for the moment and pick up another time. If there's no request to continue, reintroduce the book when the child is older; it may have a new impact.

A number of magazines are designed to help parents enrich children's experiences, understanding of the world around them, and vocabulary. Our resource section lists several, with addresses.

Because a child draws from his receptive vocabulary—words he has heard and seen—when he speaks or writes, the broader the variety of his sources, the richer his vocabulary will be. If your children's vocabulary is formed chiefly from conversations they've had or over-heard, they're limited to one level of usage. But if he routinely adds language from books, with a variety of styles and idiom, he has a much more elaborate arsenal of words and constructions to choose from. Moreover, semanticists tell us there's no truth to the statement, "I know what I want to say, but I can't find the words to say it." In other words, if you can't say it, you can't think it.

Good literature is carefully crafted. Words are chosen because of their connotations and denotations. The constructions are varied. Other cultures and other times are represented. Fine distinctions, allusions, imagery, and multiple levels of meaning, all but absent from spoken conversation, are plentiful on the printed page.

Literature can also impose structure. "Content determines what readers think about when they are absorbed in a book, but structure determines *how* they will think about it," write Barbara Baskin and Karen Harris in *Books for the Gifted Child*. They continue:

> High-ability learners require demanding fare. Books should leave them with as many questions as answers, so that contemplating, analyzing, and judging continuously take place during the reading activity and for a long time afterward. . . . Stories in which time sequences are juggled, different characters take on the role of narrator, and unusual speech patterns appear require extra concentration from readers.
>
> Picture books have all the essential ingredients of any literary experience. At their best, the language is rich and vital; when mediocre, it is banal and dull. An alphabet book can begin, "A is for Apple, B is for Ball," or announce, "A—Armadillo, belted and Amazonian; B—bumptious baboon." The former asks little from the reader; the latter tenders an

exciting partnership. In each of these language is at work—but in one it is also at play.

Words *can* be fun. It may be enough to learn the difference between cat-hat-sat-fat, but "Swaller-dollar-cauliflower, alley garoo" is fun as well. Picture books provide indelible images of numbers, relationships, and his surroundings that give your child the tools to define the shape and limits of his world; this may mean the difference between just surviving and thriving.

Words are the keys that unlock the child's imagination. They are the stepping-stones that trace the way into unexplored worlds. Meanwhile, they look nice on your refrigerator door. Buy a ton of Post-It notes on sale and stick words everywhere during your child's total immersion. Post fun words such as *purloin* and *virgule* and beautiful words such as *mellifluous, amber, Walla Walla, cellar door, euthanasia, and echo.*

Stop short when you hear a good new word. Say it back, write it down, look it up, hang it up. When you've done that with a word, we tell our children, you own it forever. You won't lose it and no one can take it away.

There are some books that are especially rich in collectible words. Many of the Dr. Seuss books almost read themselves—start page one and they flow so wonderfully you can't put them down. Many of the words are coined—made up—to fit the meter, which isn't all bad. Take home a dozen from the library, find the ones that appeal to your child, and buy them if you're so moved. *Hop on Pop, Fox in Sox,* and *Mr. Brown Can Moo; Can You?* are all likely candidates.

When your child finds them fun, bring in the Amelia Bedelia series. Amelia is a well-meaning but too-literal servant in a tolerant but idiomatic household. She receives instructions in conversational idiom and follows them literally, through several easy-to-read and fun-to-imagine episodes. Kids love them because they're conspiratorial; they realize that in English we don't always say what we mean.

William Steig is a wonderfully adept writer and illustrator. His words do not seem to be written for children, yet they have great appeal for youngsters. In *Solomon the Rusty Nail* Steig writes, "Solomon not being where he just went disconbobulated the cat. He kept circulating that tree, clockwise, counterclockwise, and otherwise, trying to find his rabbit. He finally staggered off, feeling brainsick."

Watch, too, for fun dictionaries for kids and for Workman Publishing's series of calendars consisting of 365 new or unusual words padded in tear-off pages.

Encourage your child to use a variety of words. Sometimes she'll delight you with an innovative connection: "A dragon looks like a dinosaur plus an alligator," said Lisa, just turned 3. When her brother was 4 and accompanying their mom shopping for vegetables, he told her, "*You* can eat asparagus, I'll eat a spare tire."

Reward them. Let them know it's important to come up with original expressions. Write them on your calendar/log/baby book, and when the chemistry is right, leave a tape recorder running to capture the constructions of the moment. Dub little snatches of conversation onto an audio log on a longer cassette. Be sure to date the entries, because this may well become an irreplaceable keepsake, to say nothing of evidence for qualifying for special enrichment or enhancement programs.

As you read, remember that the child who learns to love books will want to read. Venerable child development expert Bruno Bettelheim concludes that "reading is not just a tool, the use of which can be learned any which way, the faster and easier the better." Rather, he continues, we must emphasize the significance of reading to those readers at either end of the spectrum—both gifted and poor readers.

Here are some picture books recommended by Barbara Baskin and Karen Harris in *Books for the Gifted Child* as especially appropriate for challenging gifted children in the preschool and early elementary grades:

Aardema, Verna:	*Who's in Rabbit's House?*
Adamson, George:	*Finding 1 to 10*
Anno, Mistumasa:	*Anno's Alphabet: An Adventure in Imagination*
	Anno's Journey
	Topsy-Turvies: Pictures to Stretch the Imagination
Baskin, Leonard:	*Hosie's Alphabet*
	Hosie's Aviary
DePaola, Tomie:	*Helga's Dowry*
Gwynne, Fred:	*A Chocolate Moose for Dinner*
	The King Who Rained
Kennedy, Richard:	*The Porcelain Man*
Lisker, Sonia O.:	*I Used to* (for kindergarten age)
Seuss, Dr.:	*On Beyond Zebra*

BEGINNING TO READ

The literature and the parents' lounges are filled with stories of youngsters who surprised everyone by reading without any formal lessons.

One gifted girl at 18 months showed an interest in the alphabet. After two months of learning with her mother she knew all the letters and the numbers 1-14. She began to recite books to her parents, having learned them by rote, appropriately including when to turn the pages.

Gifted toddlers will sometimes slip into learning the alphabet and reading children's books and street signs on their own almost without anyone knowing it, especially if they are raised in an environment that encourages reading and provides nonpressured opportunities for it. One study, described by Donald C. Cushenbery and Helen Howell in *Reading and the Gifted Child: A Guide for Teachers*, showed that one-third to one-half of children later identified as gifted were reading before the first day of kindergarten. (We would caution that the other half to two-thirds were no less gifted.) Provide the early opportunity and nurture the early signs but don't pressure. Even some experts who adamantly oppose teaching of reading to preschoolers believe child-initiated early reading should be nurtured.

WHEN YOUR CHILD BEGINS TO WRITE

After your little one has filled himself up with ideas and their spoken expressions, words, sooner or later some of them are going to spill out in something other than speech. Perhaps you've already noticed something. Sometimes her doodles on paper (or in the air) are long lines of waveforms, or long barbed wire strings of loops. Or rows of slash marks. It doesn't take much imagination to see that these are imitations of cursive writing. Having seen you write all along, she's rehearsing for a little writing of her own.

Actually she's capable of language composition long before her hands and fingers are ready to write. Just as spoken language came along before people started to inscribe symbols, she has been composing little blurbs of her own for some time. Let her dictate these to you and you'll have a record that you can play back to her on the spot and later.

Back to the chalkboard in the kitchen. Inventory the words she "owns." Write large and let her copy below. Go long on praise, short on correction; there's time for that later. You'll get inversions; don't worry, they're normal. Display a balance of the words she already knows; capture new ones; mix with pictures and squiggles if she wants, but keep it *fun*.

Her first writing will be a mixture of copied letters, blobs, stars, hash marks, and whatever comes to mind. Then she will start to use letters as symbols for something else. You'll hear her saying the words she's trying to write—feeling how her mouth makes the sound, and going for the letters—usually consonants at first. Now she'll bring you her treasures. Be full of praise for her efforts. Resist the temptation to make all the letters capitals or lowercase. Overlook the reversed letters, phonetic spelling, lack of spaces, and transpositions. That will come later, and your child will be her own toughest critic soon enough.

If your child has an older sibling who's a gifted perfectionist, take him aside and stress the importance of tolerance. Conversely, there's nothing like praise from an idolized older child to encourage hard work at building skills.

What older children don't realize, but parents do and Piaget did, is that younger children reinvent language every day. They have heard language all along, and without being given formal structural demonstrations, they have discovered language's underlying order. They have picked up certain rules that you and I probably couldn't even put into words. These are indigenous to English, a language that's about as irregular as you could hope to find anywhere in the world. In fact, children tend to overregularize our language, for instance, treating irregular verbs as though they were regular and saying "I brang it to school" or "He slud into third base." The child is figuring out the scheme of English every time he hears our constructions. That's why it helps him to hear English modeled at home, in discussions of ideas, morals, history. He is using this overlay of rules as he puts his own words and sentences together.

The child writes first for himself. As his only critic, he's universally accepting. Later he gets a sense of the audience, and he begins to see his work as someone else will see it. That's when conventions such as punctuation and spelling will become more important.

"Around the age of seven," writes Cammie Atkins in an article in the journal *Young Children*,

children gradually realize that other people may not see their writing as they do. . . . Where *process* had been all important, now the *product* takes precedence. As this happens children's attitude toward writing becomes more serious.

The complement to child as active learner is adult as guide and facilitator. As they experiment with writing, children need supportive adults. They need adults to provide the tools needed for writing and the time and opportunity to use those tools. They need adults to ensure an atmosphere conducive to exploration and to good feelings about writing. They need adults to accept what is written as worthwhile, and to appreciate the work and effort that goes into learning to write. And, children especially need adults who understand that the errors they made are an important part of the learning process, not something bad that should be red-marked and criticized.

Finally, both child writers and the adults supporting them must practice patience. Writing takes time. Any given piece involves continuous interplay of many elements—thinking, writing, reading, rethinking, rewriting, rereading, and so forth. Patience is needed to allow this process to unfold. Writing is a process. It cannot be hurried, it cannot be forced. It must be nurtured and encouraged. It must be appreciated. After all, it is a remarkable thing children do when they write!

Creativity: It's All in Your Head

Like the Abominable Snowman and the Loch Ness Monster, the quality we call *creativity* has undergone a serious scientific search. In this book, we don't offer a revolutionary theory of creativity because we don't have one. However, before this chapter ends, we will examine what has been said about creativity by a number of respected people who are devoting their entire professional lives to the study of child development, the mind, and the realization of human potential. We try to offer a sense of what makes up creative behavior and some of the conditions that are believed to encourage its development.

Barbara Clark, of California State University at Los Angeles, is one of the most prolific and insightful writers and teachers in the field. In the 1988 edition of her encyclopedic work *Growing Up Gifted* she draws from every conceivable source; her bibliography is fifty-three pages long. If your library has one of the earlier editions or none at all, ask them to order the new one.

Clark begins by declaring that creativity is "the highest expression of giftedness," integrating the four commonly identified functions of the mind:

- Thinking: rational thinking, the aspect of creativity easiest to measure through tests and develop through conscious practice.

- Feeling: self-awareness, self-actualization, with a high degree of emotional energy.
- Sensing: a state of talent, with high levels of physical or mental development, and a high level of skill in a specific talent.
- Intuiting: higher level of consciousness, use of imagery, fantasy; involves a breakthrough to preconscious or unconscious levels.

1. THINKING AND CREATIVITY

Let's begin by considering the first of these components, rational thinking. It is the most readily measured by testing and for some researchers the first and last place to look for creative behavior. Many experts, including E. Paul Torrance, professor emeritus from the University of Georgia, and J. P. Guilford, past president of the American Psychology Association and creator of the Guilford Structure of Intellect model, concur that there are four main aspects of creative thinking:

- Fluency, the ability to produce many ideas or possibilities on a given topic. An example is brainstorming, a process in which a group of people all contribute randomly the ideas that come to mind on a common topic. For example, how many ways can you think of to use a Styrofoam cup?
- Flexibility, the ability to see things in a new way, to try different approaches. There are "brainteasers," puzzles and story problems that require children to seek new perspectives.
- Originality, the ability to come up with a unique or original idea or response. For example, when students continued to vandalize school plumbing fixtures, a consultant we know suggested a "June School-wide Pizza Party Fund," from which, students were told, plumbing repair funds would be deducted. Money left over would buy pizza. The vandalism dropped dramatically; the students had a great party *and* the school cut maintenance expenses more than $10,000 in the first year.
- Elaboration, the ability to take a basic idea and expand on it. If the idea is to replace the internal combustion engine with an alternative

power supply, several repercussions would follow. List the consequences and trace their subsequent effects on the economy, the environment, and our life-style.

SOWING THE SEEDS OF CREATIVITY

Research indicates that the rational thinking aspect of creativity is an acquired behavior and therefore can be learned and enhanced with guidance and practice. Two often-used tests of creative thinking are the Minnesota Tests of Creative Thinking (MTCT) and the Torrance Tests of Creative Thinking.

Do intelligence tests identify creative students? Not necessarily; in a given population there are probably some intellectually gifted children of average creativity, some creatively gifted who are in the normal IQ ranges; and some who score high on both. After a program of creative thinking exercises, many students can earn higher scores on the creativity tests. (We have to acknowledge that this might mean they have learned *strategies for taking creativity tests*.)

Just as you prepare your child for communicating by making tools and techniques readily available, we feel you can encourage him to be creative by helping him think through the steps of the creative process.

Children must learn to examine the assumptions behind a particular situation before seeking solutions:

- Fact-finding: define the status quo.
- Problem finding: what is the source?
- Idea finding: name all the alternatives.
- Solution finding: which alternative would solve the problem?
- Acceptance finding: can we make this alternative work?
- Plan of action: how can we make the change?

Encourage critical and creative thinking by showing your children hands-on problem solving. When your children come to you for a solution to a problem, don't be too quick to mediate; turn the problem into an opportunity. Ask them to describe the situation and brainstorm for new ideas. Look for divergent thinking and lots of ideas and solutions.

When they describe a problem, get them to break it down—what is actually happening?

Once they have identified the problem, go for the facts. What goes wrong when?

Now help them look for as many alternatives as they can think of. Replace every factor of the problem with one or more alternatives. Consider the effects of each. Encourage wholly radical departures from the status quo. (Five kids must share three apples equally; they make applesauce. Two siblings must share a piece of cake. They agree that one will cut two equal pieces, but the other may have first choice.)

Next, evaluate every idea. Find the ones most likely to be effective with the least cost or impact and the highest reliability.

Then prepare to put the new plan into effect. This may involve some "selling" of the plan to others; they may have to pave the way for a compromise, seek permission for an intrusion, float a loan, gain access to a space, borrow tools, ask to waive a rule or deadline.

This process is really no different from what people do when they need to be more effective, whether in business, school, church, or volunteer organizations. Look around. Perhaps you now know, or remember from your own childhood, a person who was particularly adept at pulling things off. Reread the steps above. Was he using this technique? Would you call him creative, or effective, or both?

We know a highly effective teacher of gifted preschoolers who has devised her own methods for settling disputes between classmates. She seats the parties at a round table called the "peace table," where they sit down as equals to puzzle out the problems. "What do you two think is best?" "How can we avoid a situation like this?" "Here are the choices; talk them over and let me know your decision."

"They get caught up in doing things together," she told us. "We have never had a negative response; they always come up with a solution. It's a fantastic technique in discipline; they look at new ways to do things in a positive and reinforcing manner. They enjoy being able to deal with frustrations. We're careful to praise our children for all their accomplishments; then they feel wonderful and they know they can do it."

Robert Eberle, the late Creative Education Foudation colleague and Illinois school administrator, developed this memory training technique in *Visual Thinking: A "Scamper" Tool for Useful Imaging* to help children remember the steps in fluent, flexible, and elaborate thought:

S	SUBSTITUTE	To have a person or thing act or serve in the place of another: Who else instead? What else? Other place? Other time?
C	COMBINE	To bring together, unite: How about a blend, an assortment? Combine purposes? Combine ideas?
A	ADAPT	To adjust for the purpose of suiting a condition or purpose: What else is like this? What other ideas does this suggest?
M	MODIFY	Alter, change form or quality; change meaning, color, motion, sound, odor, taste, form.
	MAGNIFY	Enlarge, make great in form or quality: What to add? Greater frequency? Stronger? Larger?
	MINIFY	Make smaller, lighter, slower, less frequent: What to subtract? Smaller? Lighter? Slower? Split up? Less frequent?
P	PUT TO OTHER USES	New ways to use it? Other uses if modified?
E	ELIMINATE	To remove, omit, get rid of a part, quality, or whole: What parts can be taken out? To keep the same function? To change the function?
R	REVERSE	To place opposite or contrary, to turn it around: Opposites? Turn it backwards? Turn it upside down? Turn it inside out?
	REARRANGE	To change order, or adjust; different plan, layout or scheme: Other sequence? Change pace?

University of Chicago and Northwestern University Professor of Education Benjamin Bloom's taxonomy of the cognitive domain is often used to demonstrate how thinking skills may be taught and can be helpful to parents of preschoolers. For example, suppose you and your child are preparing a space for her to use as a garden. The following factors would come into play:

- Knowledge: the information she finds about plants from books, parents, or other sources.
- Comprehension: she chooses plants for her space.
- Application: she plots out the garden and plants and cares for it.
- Analysis: she sketches plan views of the garden, collects plants and insects, sees the effect of fertilizer, and charts seedlings' progress on a time line or calendar.
- Synthesis: she relates her garden to other aspects of plant and animal life: books, grocery-store produce section, and public gardens.
- Evaluation: she uses this year's experience to plan whether and how to continue with a garden next year, possibly with seeds harvested from this year's crop.

Margie Kitano applies Bloom's taxonomy to kindergarten art in her article "Young Gifted Children: Strategies for Preschool Teachers" published in *Young Children* (May 1982). Using the example of awareness of colors, Kitano supplies this hypothetical dialogue:

> What color is this? (Knowledge)
> How do we get the color green? (Comprehension)
> Paint a picture using primary and secondary colors. (Application)
> How does this picture make you feel? What colors did the painter use
>   to make you feel that way? (Analysis)
> Paint a picture that conveys the feeling of anger. (Synthesis)
> How effective is the use of color in this picture? (Evaluation)

Torrance himself set down ten recommendations for setting the stage for creativity growth in a flyer circulated by the National Association for Gifted Children:

1. Provide materials that develop imagination, such as open-ended stories or drawings.
2. Provide materials that enrich imagery, such as fairy tales, folktales, myths, fables, nature books.
3. Permit time for thinking and daydreaming. Just because a child does not look like he is busy does not mean that his mind is not.

4. Encourage children to record their ideas in binders, notebooks, etc. Even playing secretary for your child by having him dictate stories and ideas can be a special way of showing that his ideas are valuable and that you care what he is thinking.
5. Encourage your child to take a different look at things. There are many things one can learn about the world by standing on one's head!
6. Encourage true individuality. Find little details about your child's work or behavior that show you see him as a special person.
7. Be cautious in editing a child's products. Find ways to make him feel the worth of being a creator.
8. Encourage your child to play with words. Use word games such as rhyming, opposites, and puns to their full advantage.
9. Learn and reinforce some of the specific thinking processes that go into the creative act.
10. Provide opportunities for your child to sense problems and create possible solutions.

2. FEELINGS AND CREATIVITY

For a seed to sprout and grow, it needs certain conditions—light, water, soil, nutrients. Anything less yields a lower return or nothing at all. No less is true of creativity. Given less than optimal surroundings, wonderful things may still happen, but probably in a far smaller percentage of situations.

The environment that encourages the development of potential creativity is one of safety, where the child has self-confidence and basic trust and feels at home. Parents and teachers discourage creativity when they belittle a child, laugh at his silly thoughts, remind him that he's inadequate, discourage risk taking, and let him know they expect precise, productive, and logical performance at all times. On the other hand, if you'd prefer to nurture creative thought, our advice would be to encourge risk taking, accept near-misses, promote his self-reliance, and *help him learn to accept failure*, because there will undoubtedly be some of that along the way.

The gifted child's own perfectionist tendencies may lead to a preference for staying on the safe side. Nothing ventured, nothing lost. Also, the "gifted" label may make him doubly cautious lest he be ridiculed for failing to meet others' high expectations. Teachers, by the way, can add to this difficulty, with comments such as, "If you're supposed to be gifted, why can't you figure out this problem." When these comments are made in front of classmates, it's like declaring open season on the gifted child, who may already feel animosity from peers. At these times, it's essential for the gifted child to have an inner reserve that enables him to have self-directed goals and self-evaluated results.

As we foster such inner security we have to balance the comfort of safety with the challenge of advancement. Even if we don't love change ourselves, our children must learn to welcome it. A useful book, *What Do You Really Want for Your Children?* by Wayne Dyer, urges us to help our children feel in total control of themselves and to view fears and wariness as self-imposed limitations.

Dyer continues that a child must learn how to fail, to accept failing at a task and not confuse it with failing as a person.

> We must begin to teach our children that failing is not only acceptable, but that it is an absolute requirement if they want to be no-limit people.....
>
> Young people who are afraid of failing are usually obsessed with achievement. They tend to evaluate their personal worth and success in terms of external achievement . . . inner rewards are considered meaning-less. Instead it is the money, the trophy, the diploma that really have meaning.

Dyer on creativity: "It is my very strong belief that all children are creative, and that we encourage or discourage that natural creativity by the ways in which we relate to children."

He lists seven central ingredients, with parenthetical guidelines, of a creative approach to raising children:

1. A sense of independence.
2. An absence of labels.
3. Personal integrity (being honest with oneself, feeling at peace with oneself even when one makes mistakes, and receiving praise for telling the truth, that is, not being punished for honesty).

4. Never fearing one's own greatness (not seeing heroes as more significant than oneself, but considering heroes as examples of what the child can achieve).
5. Intensity of awareness (support the intensity of their involvement with their games and fantasies. "They should find excitement and praise in your eyes when they develop their own skits and games. The intensity of those creations will flow naturally into their later endeavors.").
6. Persistence ("Help them not to give up, ever, on the things that are of great importance to them. Help them to never think in impossibility terms, and to see the value of staying with a situation until it is resolved.").
7. Independence in thought (encourage questioning; teach them to question conventional wisdom and come up with their own theories . . . be open minded, nonjudgmental).

Dyer also lists his characteristics of the creative child:

- Loves to play and invent new games.
- Asks "why" all the time.
- Doesn't censor his own ideas, but expresses them.
- Is willing to take sensible risks.
- Often prefers to learn or work alone.
- Finds "toys" everywhere.
- Loves puzzles, building blocks, mazes, toys that challenge him to make his unique mind work overtime.
- Loves to experiment and try new things.
- Wears his emotions clearly on his face.
- Loves new situations.
- Is not prejudiced and doesn't join cliques.
- Learns very quickly from his mistakes.
- Has a sense of humor.

You may appreciate a story, perhaps apocryphal, about a cub reporter assigned to get the secret of success from a veteran statesman. "My secret? Good judgment," offered the statesman. Nothing like the 1,200 words the reporter had to fill. "How do you get good judgment?" he countered. "Experience," came the reply. No quitter, the reporter asked the obvious: "How did you get experience?" "Bad judgment." End of interview. End of lesson.

3. TALENT AND CREATIVITY

Imagination is a key element of creative talent. Well beyond synthesis, which relies on combining existing factors into an innovative combination, creative talent begins with a viewpoint, a state of mind, a condition, and produces something new that is a product of some or all of those elements.

The creative person is directed by an inner sense of values; public acclaim will not make up for the creator's dissatisfaction with an effort. Conversely, criticism can't shake the confident artist. There lies the distinction between an artist and an entertainer. Further, creative individuals will look at things and issues from all sides; experiment with media; stretch assignments past the limits; thrive in controversial situations rather than shrink from conflict; and feel free to voice divergent, unorthodox, outlandish opinions. They may throw themselves into an argument with great relish, as partisans wholly devoted to one side or the other, only to speak just as convincingly for the opposing view a day later.

To develop your child's talent, we refer you to *Developing Talent in Young People*, written by Benjamin Bloom and his research team, the benchmark study of encouragement, determination, challenge and reward in childhood, and the effect of parenting styles among 120 "immensely talented" individuals in theoretical, psychomotor, and artistic fields. Although it is clear that the home atmospheres were vital to the framework of these careers, this book makes no effort to tell you what you should do with your children. It does, however, identify the correlations among the families it interviewed, and they can be compelling.

Among the common factors discovered by Bloom's team were the following: first experiences with the skills being studied were fun and recreational; first teachers were full of praise but short on pedagogic technique; homes were positive and encouraging environments; parents were supportive and—as these world-class talents developed—sacrificial in their support, sometimes to the detriment of siblings and family welfare.

4. INTUITION AND CREATIVITY

The child with strong intuitive powers may also be more advanced than others. Encourage daydreams, fantasy, and imaginative enterprises. Expose him to other cultures, philosophies, times, and frames of reference through literature. Myths, fables, and fairy tales all contribute.

A common attribute of creatively gifted children is an ability to see beyond the concrete and tangible. The ability to understand abstractions is one of the first evidences of giftedness reported by parents. A perfect example is time, a purely abstract convention invented by humans to explain abstract concepts. The child who links events, makes connections, and comprehends and deals with ideas such as eight more days until her birthday, an event the day before yesterday, and what it means to be 4½ has a head start toward more elaborate concepts ahead.

Literature is wonderful for stretching concepts, because it can dance along and over the line between concrete and abstract. When imagination comes into play, the child's mind can deal with complicated theories in bite-size, manageable chunks. People who grew up listening to Fibber McGee open his closet on his weekly radio program know the power of the spoken word to evoke imaginary images in a way that television and movies cannot hope to equal. Although nostalgic rebroadcasts are popular in some cities, radio drama is hard for most people to find these days.

Fortunately, books read aloud have most of the same effect, especially for younger children who aren't yet accomplished readers. As we emphasized in the previous chapter, there is no substitute for time spent reading aloud to young children. For the specific aspect of giftedness we call creativity, there is no more reliable exercise your child can find than listening to you read.

Mary Poppins, with her metaphysical abilities, is a good starter exercise, just a short leap from Frosty the Snowman and The Grinch. The Poppins book, records, and the movie are all readily available.

When they are ready, a good early exercise for children is C. S. Lewis's story of The Lion, The Witch, and The Wardrobe, in which children step into a wooden clothes wardrobe and thence into quite another world, Narnia, where animals speak and trees are animated and quite protective of certain people. Many children who hear or read *Wardrobe* become hooked on the concept and sign on for the entire seven-volume series, *Chronicles of Narnia*. Like many works of lasting value, the Narnia books are richly allegorical, and invite rereading and appreciation at various levels.

Like Lewis, Madeleine L'Engle writes about families who move in and out of these times and this place. Firmly based in natural sciences, she moves comfortably into the metaphysical world where sensitive people live in empathetic harmony with dolphins and establishment scientists unlock the mystery of travel through time. These books are as naturally captivating to intellectually curious children as they were off-putting to the cautious editors who declined to print *A Wrinkle in Time*, her initial step into paraphysical matters. Once a publisher could be found, it sold wonderfully and was winner of the Newberry Award for that year, 1961.

L'Engle recalled the long road to publication with Studs Terkel on his WFMT, Chicago, radio program:

When I wrote *A Wrinkle in Time* I wasn't thinking about any age level; I was writing about some things that fascinated me. . . . I thought it was a terrific book. I was not prepared for two years of rejection slips. It's a rather difficult book for many grownups. So these editors would read it, and not understand it, and they would assume that children could not understand it.

When my present publisher, Farrar, Straus, and Giroux, finally took it, *they* assumed it couldn't be read below high school level. They said, "Well, dear, we don't expect this book to sell well; we're doing it as sort of a self-indulgence, so we don't want you to be disappointed when it doesn't sell." So when it took off like a skyrocket they were totally [exasperated] about it.

Well, my kids were 7, 10 and 12 when I was writing it, and I was reading it to them at bedtime and [then] I would go back to the typewriter. So I knew kids could understand it . . . and the kids had no problem whatsoever. First of all, they were interested in the story. As long as the story carries them on. A published writer . . . said to me, "When I was about 10, I read *A Wrinkle in Time*. I didn't understand it but I knew what it was about." That's a marvelous way of saying it; the kids know what it's about.

Regarding children's ability to tackle complicated ideas, L'Engle says,

First of all, I never write for children; I write for myself. I don't believe that books should be slotted—pigeonholed and stuck into age levels. They're for people who like to read. And if they're about the human predicament—about what people are concerned with—there isn't any age limit. Dickens wrote for people. I read *David Copperfield* when I was 8 or 9.

Fortunately, Vicky's mother [in *A Ring of Endless Light*] doesn't say, "when you're old enough, you'll understand," because first of all we never will understand; we just need to go on asking more questions. The point is to find the right questions to ask and not be limited by finite, tight, rigid little answers.

L'Engle often deals with the conflict between the positive and the dark side of human nature. Her characters face and deal with complicated issues of real life. Like the author, they are grounded with an abiding faith, which gives them strength, and they take chances that carry the risk of failure—an important model for children who will make similar decisions. L'Engle's style is wonderfully narrative, especially rich in imagery and possessing a distinctive cadence that begs to be read aloud, almost as though it was spoken first and transcribed to paper later.

All this reading aloud will perhaps foster some profound thinking. It is most helpful to have islands of quiet time and space in your child's life. Even in a large family or crowded quarters, time alone and space for contemplation are critically important.

FOSTERING CREATIVE LEARNING

By now you may already have thought of half a dozen ways you might nurture your child's creativity in the day-to-day activities you and your family already enjoy. Begin immediately, and be on the lookout for more!

Here are a few starter ideas that may lead you to your own:

- Encourage storytelling. Take turns contributing to a common plot; use a timer to signal when it's the next person's turn. In the car, you may want to use a certain landmark or the odometer reading as a timekeeper.
- Don't interrupt a child deeply involved in a creative activity. Try to keep a place where she can leave work in progress, mess and all.

- Build some air into schedules where possible, short of legalizing anarchy. Meals and bedtime should come at fixed times, all things being equal, but otherwise try to be flexible.

- Look for ways to integrate subjects. Keep your antennae out for connections, bridges, parallels, and ask pointed questions to help her trace the connections. (When that fails, go ahead and hit her over the head with them.)

- Provide a large variety of working materials—including things you were about to discard: egg cartons, plastic trays, papers, cardboard boxes, string and tape, empty rolls from paper towels, twist ties from bread, felt squares, leftovers from printing projects. Ask a friendly printer for the ends of rolls of continuous web paper. (Don't tell them we sent you.) Watch for companies that change names or logos, or add partners, or change addresses. Sometimes they'll discard tons of fine bond stationery, and for a couple of dollars your neighborhood printer might trim off the printed part at the end of a shift. Sometimes your best work deserves a watermarked bond.

- Allow the child to help plan your trips; be wide open to suggestions on routes, side trips, food, and distance. While traveling, encourage wide-ranging discussions. They make the time and miles fly.

- Regardless of the number of children you have or jobs you hold down, there is no substitute for time alone with each child as frequently as you can manage.

- Encourage imaginative play with ordinary household items. One gifted 4-year-old held an imaginary class in her nightly bath. Her pupils were empty shampoo and dishwashing soap bottles. Each class member was identified by name and had a distinct personality. (Class size was finally limited by her mother when the bottle collection exceeded thirty pieces and threatened to take over the entire bathroom.)

- Encourage all suggestions and ideas; don't criticize, but rather ask for elaboration, and give full attention and help to the ideas your child shares.

- Whenever possible allow your child full access to kitchen, workshop, garage, or work areas.

- Visit libraries often; know your way around their collections; make yourself known to the staff. Watch for new acquisitions, prints, games, artwork, and software.

- Encourage original models and "junk sculptures" from found objects instead of plastic model kits with cut-and-dried directions that overrule creativity. (When the kits come as gifts, at least encourage your child to paint or embellish them in a divergent way.)

- Keep activities modest enough to be completed with positive attitudes—challenging but attainable.

- Don't compare one child's creative work with another's.

- Encourage and expand your child's interests, but watch for signs of fatigue and be ready to stop or move on to a new area.

- Let your child know you trust her to do what is reasonable and responsible. This trust is essential before the child can take risks.

TWO CREATIVE GIRLS: LIZ AND SARAH

The stories of two girls' childhood are worth considering as we prepare to deal with our own children's creative side. LeoNora Cohen of the Talented and Gifted Institute, University of Oregon at Eugene, wrote a memoir she calls "Indian Summer," about their recent summer when Native American lore dominated her daughter Liz's thoughts. Then a young woman named Sarah described for us her imagination, which she feels sustains her in adulthood even though it was not always encouraged in her childhood.

Liz's mother writes:

> Even before Liz could walk, she was happiest when outside, exploring ants and moss in the cracks in the sidewalk. Just after her third birthday, she asked us to leave her in the woods by herself so she could discover the wonders under each rock. At four, she declared, "These mushrooms will turn blue when I put them in water and mud," and she carried out the experiment.
>
> The summer of 1986 was Indian Summer for Liz, who was then seven. Books on Native Americans had captured her fantasies. She insisted she had the soul of an Indian, as she felt reverent toward nature. She was moved by the Iroquois' prayer to the deer or tree before killing it or cutting it. She insisted we dig up all the roots of our family tree to find Indian

blood. It was tricky, having a Russian-Brazilian and Polish background, but we established a land bridge theory, so this little girl was satisfied.

She wanted to make a teepee. Her dad helped her find, strip, and lash together eight ten-foot poles with sheets decorated with Indian symbols. She made a shelter in the woods all by herself, weaving sticks between a cluster of trees, layering leafed branches, covering them with soil and leaves. In it she hung talismans that would be important to an Indian—a jay's feather, a corn cob, a dead salamander she found on the road. She found a grinding stone and a flat stone with a hollow and spent days grinding popcorn into meal and flour. She made jerked venison, quite a project in July when hunting season doesn't start until November, after learning to cure the meat over a smoky fire; she faithfully tended it for about 24 hours.

Children need freedom to pursue their themes through interests. Often we impose too much on them; we worry about waste of time. While I am in no way opposed to planned activities like camp, lessons, and field trips, in the right doses, we must learn to listen to our children's needs and grant them more autonomy to control their worlds. We can *scaffold*, providing an outside framework that *supports* development.

Finally, an account of Sarah's childhood experiences in her own words:

All children love to read, right? Wrong. I didn't. As a two-year-old I found storybooks dull. After a few pages of tolerating them (even then I tried to be polite) I squirmed off the reader's lap, took another book, and created new, alternative plots to fit the pictures I saw. This disappointed the adults. It was ever so much more exciting to venture off into new worlds, full of wild exotic preposterous stories.

As I approached kindergarten I was talking to myself for hours, wearing odd clothes, asking questions of passersby, hiding out in neighbors' garages and spying on my folks from my favorite tree lookout. I had this strong conviction that I would find someone committing a dastardly crime that no one but myself would see, crouched so quietly in my tree, and that I would become part of a heroic band that would save a screeching victim from some horrid fate.

In my imaginings, I conducted sermons, taught school, worked as a librarian, was an honorable captain of the *Queen Elizabeth 2*, a fisherman at sea, a witch, a bird lady in the park, an orphan, a fireman and a railroad worker. My favorite pastime was saving old ladies in burning houses. I basked in their praise, as they explained to the press in long teary accounts how I had jumped through the burning window, tied up all the sheets and towels, and managed to let them down through the flames, unharmed. I was four years old, and quite content to live in a land completely my own, although this was not easy. In order to survive, I had to suppress my wild side and present a more mundane appearance.

We moved to England, to a small factory town in Yorkshire, and I found myself soaking in textures and characters that turned my imagination loose again. Chimney sweeps, window cleaners, Bobbies and midwives became my friends. Mrs. Evans, a round jovial Yorkshire woman next door, regularly invited me in for tea and shortbread.

My friend Guy and I used to run down the hill to where the trains swished by and write down the numbers on the trains. In case of robbery, we would know the number and be able to tell the authorities. We kept the numbers on little pieces of paper in a little can and never showed them to anyone!

Perhaps the saddest incident during this time was my removal from drama class. In England, theatre is part of the regular curriculum. We would all tramp up the steps for an hour of invigorating and imaginative theatre, and I looked forward to it every day. However, since starting this class, my mother claimed, I was staying up until midnight, talking to myself (more than usual) heatedly. They were exciting times, alone in the dark at night.

The problem is that grownups had no idea what I was up against. I felt like a little school girl trying to sleep while my room literally filled up with people! And very demanding people they were: I had two families, one with three children and another with two, an older man who never divulged his name but wandered all over England with a knapsack full of cans of soup (a really jolly chap), a factory worker named Harvey who never tied his shoes, and several green and ruby elves from Ireland who came to visit me only once.

Well, my parents had a conference with the school and they jointly decided that I was "over-stimulated" and should be removed from drama. I was crushed. I felt that I was being punished for having an imagination. And it was the only thing I looked forward to in school, or in my whole day.

Today I continue to talk to myself, but I have given myself the license to do so. It still amazes me how often I feel guilty for this. I am lucky in that I am winning the battle. Imagination makes all the difference between hope and despair.

Last winter I was trudging through snow with a friend. She was complaining about the weather, having to tramp through this horrid stuff, what a bore the train was, and the drudgery of travelling every day. I just said, "I don't mind at all, because I'm imagining that I've been in a ghastly Siberian work camp for months, eating nothing but dry crusts and greasy broth and they've just let me go and this is the last train out of the station to freedom, warmth, and good food."

"You're a nut," she said.

And I probably am. But I am a happy nut. For children imagination is freedom, and often it is the first thing to go in school. What do children gain by giving up their imagination? Despair. Children need imagination to survive. They don't need therapy and entertainment and computer games and chocolate and VCRs. They need their own creative spirits, and if they have lost those, parents and teachers must help them find them again. My imagination is my salvation and I will hold onto it if it's the last thing I do. It is the last train out of the station, and I'm going to be on it.

6

Preschool and Primary School: When, Which One, and Even Whether

Sooner or later parents have to make some basic choices about school. We're all looking for the critical mix of content, timing, and educational philosophy. We know our children need encouragement, stimulation, and a positive and loving environment, but where, how, and when?

Parents' natural desire to have the best for their children carries over into education, but sometimes for the worst reasons. In some keeping-up-with-the-Joneses neighborhoods you may hear that you absolutely *must* get your child enrolled in a particular preschool. Don't be fooled. If the preschool were to close on Friday would the community become a ghost town by next Monday? Of course not. Life would go on. Parents also get the message that if they don't enroll their child in half a dozen classes they are neglecting his talent and stunting his emotional and mental development. Nonsense. What's right for your child depends on his learning style, strengths, development, and the mix of formal and informal sources of enrichment in your community. No book can tell you exactly what will work with your child in your neighborhood. What we hope to do is equip you to find out enough about your child and your schools to make some considered judgments.

Among the decisions facing parents are when to start outside schooling (age 3? 4? 5?) and what type of school to choose (public? parochial? private? other?).

First, regarding preschool. Most preschools are good at what they do; if you know what they do you won't be disappointed. They are not mandatory. You needn't feel guilty if your child doesn't get into the "best" one. You don't even have to give excuses if you don't *try* to.

Cradles of Eminence, the Goertzel & Goertzel book describing the early childhood environment of many of this century's eminent public figures, is full of home schooling, parent-mentors, late school entry, and everything but preschools. You needn't feel you're depriving your child if you don't find a preschool program that fits her needs.

Barbara Clark writes in the third edition of *Growing Up Gifted* that

> The more planned educational experiences a child over three has, the better that child does in intellectual, language, personal and social development—significantly better than children placed in programs focused on free play . . . Remember that the most important thing in early learning is not the information taught, but the processes learned and the attitudes developed. Developing the intellectual ability of children truly means helping them to develop physically, emotionally, socially, cognitively, and intuitively.

We feel that the home is an entirely appropriate setting for these "planned educational experiences." The parent who is able to provide a nourishing environment in the context of our earlier chapters need not feel pressured to supplement what is already being done with outside programs. A number of factors would indicate a special need that nursery school could provide for:

- younger siblings who divert parents' attention
- need for interaction with other children for socialization or language exposure
- need for the parent or primary caretaker to have time to devote to other functions
- the inability to provide a proper nurturing environment with supervised activities, stimulating surroundings, or essential services.

From time to time, studies are undertaken to find out whether and what kind of advantage the nursery school graduate demonstrates as a primary student. Children from disadvantaged families show the greatest benefit from the nursery school experience. Children who were actively and thoughtfully enriched in their own homes before kindergarten were usually not distinguishable from their peers after the first months of school.

Moreover, if one year of nursery school turns out to be a wonderful experience for your child, two years won't necessarily be any better. Many experts recommend a single year for most children. Although there seems to be a trend toward two-year preschool programs, remember that nobody knows your child as well as you do. Some gifted children are ready to tackle the world at three. Others need the security of closeness to a parent, and find plenty to enrich themselves in the home.

Burton White concludes in his 1988 book, *Educating the Infant and Toddler*,

> Indeed, there is no substantial evidence of lasting benefits—social or intellectual—from any type of nursery school experience. Apparently, a child who comes from a caring, normal family will learn as much within the social and intellectual climate of her own home as she will from experiences in a good professional school during the preschool years.

Many parents make a concerted effort to provide as much enrichment as time and ingenuity allow. Also, there are many books offering ideas, springboards for art projects, and encouragement. Preschool activities abound, if you know where to look; check with community colleges, libraries, YMCAs, park districts, and neighborhood play lots. Play groups are increasingly in vogue these days; some are genuine efforts to provide peer-group experience; but others are little more than baby-sitting pools masquerading behind a more respectable euphemism. Keep your eyes and ears open and ask other parents what kinds of things are going on in your neighborhood.

Libraries, of course, are fountains of information. Hundreds of books have been written in the last decade about activities, encouragement, skills, crafts, development, and learning exercises. Some deal directly with giftedness. Rummage around. Some libraries collect such books in special racks near toddlers' play areas so parents can browse and researh without leaving their children.

We strongly recommend a thorough, comparative look at any pre-school you're considering. Barbara Clark offers a concise checklist of what you should be watching for:

The Teachers
    How do they interact with the children?
    Do they genuinely like them?
    Are they authentic, or do they speak in patronizing, chirpy voices?

Do they ask known-answer or open-ended questions?
Do they listen to the answers?

The Environment
Is it thoughtful, attractive, colorful, interesting?
Is it flexible?

The Activities
Are there many different activities at different levels of difficulty to challenge all?
Do they challenge all four domains of integrative education (thinking, feeling, intuition, and physical sensing)?

There is no substitute for visiting the classroom in action. Don't go only on parents' visiting day. Watch a normal class in progress. Listen for the exchanges between adults and children. How do the children treat each other? What's the feeling in the halls? How do the children walk when they come in to begin the day? When they leave?

Keep in mind too that you should browse with one child in mind. A situation in which your elder child thrived may be a disaster for his brother. A teacher who is great with ninety-five percent of the kids he deals with is of little help if your child is among the other five percent.

Be wary of self-imposed labels or slogans. You can't be sure whether the Hickory Lane Preschool for Intellectually Advantaged Youngsters just adopted a groundbreaking new curriculum model or merely hired an ad agency.

Quite apart from stated goals and marketing handouts, the people who make everything come together for the students deserve close scrutiny. Teacher, author-editor, and consultant Rita Haynes Blocksom in her article "Preschool Gifted Programs" published in *Illinois Council for the Gifted Journal* (1985) formulated a list of qualities to watch for in teachers of gifted children:

1.   High-level intelligence.
2.   High-level commitment to early gifted students and programs.
3.   Good self-concept and emotional stability.
4.   Awareness of community resources and the ability to use them.
5.   Ability to work with parents in cooperative effort.

Blocksom lists a number of teaching techniques that don't work well with gifted children. If the school you're evaluating seems to have this kind of procedure, we suggest you look further.

Schools to avoid commit these oversights (adapted from Blocksom):

1. Use lots of work sheets. (These call for the simplest skills and do not encourage more complex thought.)
2. Use the "more of the same" approach. (Early gifted children learn earlier or more rapidly than their peers and are easily bored by repetition.)
3. Have only teacher-led discussions.
4. Insist on group activities.
5. Are negative or critical of student effort.
6. Keep materials out of the reach of children.
7. Insist on quiet at all times.
8. Are limited to desk activities.
9. Have bare walls and sterile displays.
10. Discourage visitors to the classroom.
11. Allow students to criticize the work of others.
12. Discourage attempts at fantasy and imagination.

On the other hand, a school you'd probably feel comfortable with would show you lots of the following measures (also adapted from Blocksom), which go hand in hand with gifted students and their learning styles:

1. Offer open-ended opportunities in which multiple answers/options are acceptable.
2. Introduce new concepts; bring in ideas and materials from outside the classroom.
3. Encourage (but do not insist upon) participation. (Even the very young gifted need time to pause and reflect, to complete one train of thought before going on to another.)
4. Offer independent study, allow for individual learning styles, and provide specific opportunities for individuals.
5. Are positive, accepting, open-minded.
6. Make blank paper and writing utensils available AT ALL TIMES.
7. Make allowances for some noise during group projects;
8. Provide activities in a variety of settings—tables, bookshelves, learning or resource centers, out-of-doors.

9. Have child-centered bulletin boards displaying children's works.
10. Encourage mentors, senior citizens, parents, grandparents, community volunteers to visit and assist.
11. Encourage peer praise and positive interaction.
12. Encourage creative expression, fantasy, imagination, original art, stories and other works.

An essential question is whether the person who would be your child's teacher recognizes giftedness, knows its needs, is flexible enough to encourage it, and would enjoy seeing it nurtured in your child. A gentle query, not a full-scale attack, is called for. If the teacher's eyes widen, or his voice takes on a defensive tone, keep looking at schools. If he explains that giftedness is latent until age 8, widen the scope of your search.

Watch too for freedom for the children to move around the classroom to choose activities. All children benefit from such an environment, and exercising choice teaches them to use initiative and independence. Given the ability to move on to new challenges, the child can inquire more deeply and can pace himself and learn social and democratic skills such as taking turns and sharing. "Providing a wide range of activities at varying levels of difficulty, and projects with complex and simple aspects, enables the extremely able child to choose herself an appropriate activity," concludes an unsigned feature in *Young Children* (November 1987).

One mother whose gifted children have attended various kinds of schools says this of the selection process:

> If it seems right to you, stay with it. Do not make a one-time evaluation. Keep assessing the situation. One thing you strongly disagree with does not necessarily make it bad unless the whole program is shot full with side effects.

Visit the school, but as a teacher of the gifted cautions, "no matter how fantastic the equipment or space or P.E. facilities, that is not what the child may experience. The parent's feeling of excitement may not be what the child feels." The selection process is largely an intuitive one, involving a sense of whether the school makes an effort to know the needs of each child and to balance cognitive and emotional development.

What's important is a program in which the teachers let the students know they are concerned with the student's individual worth instead of how much they know, and where teachers are positive examples to the children. Children need above all respect and a sense of self-worth. The issue of respect is inseparable from an instructional method that emphasizes higher-level thinking skills. Comments from gifted parents indicate again and again that what's most important in a school are simple human qualities of caring, inclusion, creativity, and respect. These are the aspects of schooling that children recall and draw upon later in life, long after specific lessons are forgotten.

FINDING THE RIGHT PRIMARY SCHOOLS: NOT ALWAYS AS EASY AS (K)- 1-2-3

Surely no less important than the fit between your children and their preschool program is the match you make with their first "regular" school—that is, kindergarten through third grade. When your child finishes third grade, he will have spent nearly half his life thus far there. During those four very important years children also develop feelings for school and fix their images of themselves as students.

Choosing a school district may seem at first like selecting your grandparents; it's pretty much a prearranged deal. Your kids to go the one closest to your home, right? Right, for the most part. And yet . . . you pick where that home is going to be.

Few people move once and stay put for the rest of their lives. Many have a plan to move a certain number of times as family size, income, and career either mandate or allow. Many use the occasion to find the "right" neighborhoods, and in most cases school systems are a large factor in that choice.

Dr. Janet Weeks of Northwestern University's Midwest Talent Development program advises house shoppers to look first at the high school district serving a prospective property. Read the curriculum handbook. What opportunities are available? How is it rated? Generally, good high schools inspire good feeder districts, that is, good elementary and middle schools, although the elementary systems are more subject to fluctuation because personnel and student population change more often. In such schools you're likely to be dependent on the quality of individual teachers.

Speaking at the same convocation, Weeks's colleague Joyce van-Tassel-Baska suggested a list of attributes to look for in a prospective school's philosophy, policy, or program for academically talented students:

- Self pacing: Are children able to progress in a subject at a faster rate than their age peers? Is there flexibility regarding age/grade placement, or does a child's birthday determine his grade level?
- Are able learners grouped together for special instruction? Are there multi-age groupings?
- What is teaching staff quality at subsequent levels? Knowledgeable of subject matter? Flexible and willing to group and regroup for activities? Not intimidated by able learners?
- Does the school value individuation as much as or more than socialization?
- Is there a written curriculum guide, and how is it used?
- Are there adequate support services such as counselors geared to meet the needs of gifted learners as well as those students who require special education?
- Is the administration flexible in respect to change of teacher or program for a given child?
- Is academic talent recognized and rewarded as much as athletics or musical ability?

We believe the atmosphere, purpose, and professionalism of a school deserve scrutiny. Is the classroom atmosphere positive, active, affectionate, and supportive of the child? Are moral education and development of character central to the school's mission? Are there strong support and encouragement for development of the child's individual creativity as well as for intellectual and social growth? Are parents actively involved?

TEACHERS' AND PARENTS' CHECKLIST

As you select which primary program is best for each of your children, the important choice between public and private and parochial schools should be based on as much information as possible. We asked educators and parents of gifted children to list the factors they would hope to find

in their children's primary grades. Here are the factors they would look
for:

- A view that developing giftedness is an essential mission of the
  school system.
- An emphasis on teaching children how to think rather than just
  providing information.
- Continuity in curriculum for gifted children from grade to grade,
  from primary to intermediate, from intermediate to junior high, and
  then into high school, with subject matter and its treatment coordinated at all levels.
- Assistance in transferring to other programs or other schools when
  it is appropriate.
- An organization that fosters a sense of self-worth and is willing to
  support the individual; a gentle atmosphere with caring teachers; a
  secure environment and a classroom culture that encourages imagination.
- Teachers with specialized training who can direct the children's
  learning through play; teachers who are good modelers, prac-
  titioners of the kind of instantaneous learning that takes place
  through modeling.
- An ongoing in-service program for staff.
- An activity-oriented curriculum, with teachers as facilitators who
  encourage independent thinking.
- Curriculum that includes learning by sensing, feeling, and intuiting
  as well as academic instruction.
- Flexibility in curriculum, an individualized approach, with many
  choices for children to be challenged at their various cognitive and
  developmental levels.
- Individual attention to both the children's cognitive and creative
  abilities; opportunity for individual study; and suspension of
  regular homework loads when there is extra "gifted" work.
- Balance of ability grouping and exposure to other levels. If not
  exclusively a gifted program, administrative plans should allow for
  more than one gifted child in a classroom, and there should be good
  rapport between the classroom teacher and gifted staff.
- Higher teacher-student ratios and strong financial commitment. To
  provide for proper individualized instruction, kindergartens should
  ideally have no more than twenty 5-year-olds or fifteen 4-year-olds,
  with a full-time teacher and a salaried assistant in each classroom,

and lots of supplies. Similar ratios are also ideal for primary school classes.

- Open lines of communication between parents and staff, availability of staff, opportunity to share information with principal and teachers when children enter the program so time isn't wasted mismatching the curriculum to the children's stage of development.
- Active encouragement of parental involvement.
- A program of identification that allows for parents' nomination and uses recommendations, teacher checklists, and test scores to determine eligibility.
- Evaluation of children through observation, rating scales, checklists, and tests, not to rank students but to improve instruction and learning.
- The possibility of including private tutoring as part of children's school curriculum.
- Instruction that builds children's decision-making ability and develops higher-level thinking skills, rather than eroding their confidence with continual testing and grading.
- A balance of individual and group activities to meet varying levels of social maturity.
- Character education and community spirit as part of the curriculum; clear behavior limits to encourage self-discipline; nurturance and support to foster self-confidence.

All this brings us to yet another critical decision parents face.

KINDERGARTEN: WHEN TO START?

Since the entire field of early childhood education is in a state of flux, kindergarten is receiving a great deal of attention. Should it be full day? Should reading skills be taught in kindergarten? Should entrance age be pushed up?

The first public school kindergarten in the United States was established in 1873, after the original German model. By the 1960s, Head Start and other programs increased interest in "payoffs," in showing how preschool and kindergarten programs can provide a good foundation for later academic success. By the 1980s, full-day kindergartens and public school programs including 4-year-olds were common. Working parents encourage full-day programs, and some educators feel academics should begin as early as possible. These developments have led to continued debate between proponents of child development–oriented "classic" kindergarten and educators more concerned with academic growth.

As some communities introduce advanced curricula, and others shift the cutoff age for entrance earlier or later, we parents can become confused about when to send our children to school. You could theoretically move your kindergartner, with a mid-fall birthday, to a community where her age mates would be a year ahead of or behind her. It's like crossing an international date line and losing a year.

All this can complicate the process of giving your child the optimum education. Kindergarten entry, for example, should receive more attention. Our laws make the single determinant entrance requirement the day children were born. On the first day of school, the children who show up to begin their educational careers have mental ages ranging all the way from ages 3 to 7. Among the group there are probably kids who have been reading since they were 4 and kids who are just beginning to learn English as a second language.

To us it seems unnecessarily arbitrary and confining to use a birth date as an absolute determinant. It might be adequate for the average student, but given the range we just described, it doesn't take much imagination to picture this scenario: two kids, born a week apart, find their fifth birthday approaching. One is emotionally immature but was born a week before the cutoff date, so she's going to school this year. The other child reads sixty words and is generally much more aware of the world around her, and if tested by a qualified professional would prove to be eminently deserving of the daily school experience. But the cutoff date falls between their birthdays, so the girl born a week earlier, but who is not really ready, enters school, while her 1-week-younger neighbor, ripe for the kindergarten experience, is obliged to wait one full year to get started.

Does this really happen? Yes, every September. One school told us they had made two exceptions in ten years: "One worked, the other didn't." In fact, early kindergarten entrance, when called for by examination (not just for the convenience of parents who want their days free from children's interruptions), is really nothing more than a simple act of individualizing education. The national school system in New Zealand, for example, admits children to the first year of school upon their fifth birthday, and they move freely in a multi-age K-1 atmosphere until they are ready to move ahead, *whenever that may be*. One of the New Zealand teachers, hearing about the American lockstep system, commented that ours seemed awfully unfair to the children. Some private schools circumvent the problems of lockstep grades by using other designations. Roeper City and Country School, the Bloomfield Hills, Michigan, private school for gifted students, organizes its lower school into stages. Stage I consists of 3 and 4 year olds; Stage II children are ages 4 through 7; Stage III includes 7 to 9 year olds, and Stage IV is for 8 to 11 year olds. The overlapping ages allow the children to advance from one stage to the next whenever they are ready.

Mind you, a good number of parents decide to hold their children back from kindergarten entrance so that they are a year older when they begin. This is not a bad idea; if it works for the child it's actually a good one. The question must be whether the kindergarten regimen will be too simple and repetitive for a bright 6-year-old; will he enjoy learning to recognize shapes so that he can *begin* to recognize the letters of the alphabet, or will he be sight-reading beginner books on his own by that time? Your observations will help you decide.

The Gifted and Talented Project at Teachers College of Columbia University produced a 1980 book called *Gifted Young Children* under the direction of Abraham J. Tannenbaum, a pioneering researcher-writer in the field of education of the gifted. Part of the book dealt with early entrance for certain children:

> For intellectually advanced preschool-aged children, early school entrance provides an excellent educational option. By entering school early, such children can be provided with an effective match of learning materials to readiness level, and, at the same time, experience a form of acceleration that is least disruptive to the continuity of education. It is probably far better for some children to enter school early and progress along with classmates than to enter school at a later age and experience boredom with an unchallenging curriculum or be skipped one or more grades during the course of education.

The authors continued to describe a number of studies of children who had entered school earlier than the prescribed cutoff dates, "all with generally positive results." Two studies evaluated the progress of mentally advanced children who had been admitted to school early, compared with a random sample of average children, and a group with IQs similar to the early entrants but approximately one year older. Results showed no significant differences between the early admit group and either of the other groups on achievement tests, school records, motivation, and work habits in grades 1, 3, or 7. In the fifth grade, the early admit group was rated as more highly motivated than the late admit group.

The authors go on to cite a number of research projects, all of which largely agree that early entrance has posed no special disadvantage to the children being studied (but it must be noted that children who were most at risk of failing didn't pass the screening to get into kindergarten in the first place).

Final testimony comes from David Elkind, then president of the National Association for the Education of Young Children, editor of *Young Children* magazine, and author of *The Hurried Child*, whose manifesto against excessive acceleration has inspired countless parents to cut back on intellectually ambitious programs lest they push their kids too far. In a strong editorial in *Young Children* in May 1988, he wrote:

> Promotion of intellectually gifted children is simply another way of attempting to match the curriculum to the child's abilities, not to accelerate those abilities.
> What promotion does for intellectually gifted children is to make a *better fit* between the child's level of development and the curriculum.

The goal of early entrance should be this "better fit." The only question is what is best for your child at this stage in his development. Look carefully at all your options:

A year (or additional year) of nursery school
Continuing informal learning at home, perhaps combined with a few carefully selected supplemental programs (park district lessons, swimming, music lessons, class at museums, etc.)
Private kindergarten
Public school kindergarten
Moving to another school district
Home schooling with a specific kindergarten curriculum

THE ULTIMATE PULLOUT PROGRAM: HOME SCHOOLING

For a variety of reasons, sometimes the best school simply cannot provide the individual attention your child needs. Some children need the stimulation that certain curricula provide long before they are emotionally mature enough to receive it in the classroom setting. This cannot be considered a failure of the schools. In this case, don't overlook one radical but reasonable solution, home schooling. You were her first teacher; children learn best from those they love; the home can be a wonderful atmosphere for unfolding minds. You don't necessarily have to hand over the reins to someone else the day after her fifth birthday.

Remember that the first academy was under a tree; most people learned at home before there were schools, just as everyone was born at home before there were hospitals. The most effective teaching is mentorship: one-on-one dialogue that moves as fast as the student can master the material.

Home schooling is an extreme measure, involving a sizable commitment. And, like the public, private, and parochial schools they supplant, some home schools work better than others. Of course you don't have physics labs in your basement or a 30,000-volume learning center, but if you have a good relationship with your child; if you know what makes him learn, you've got a good head start. You're already established as his first teacher; you're accustomed to setting up a learning situation; he is used to turning to you for enlightenment.

Your first step must be to research the laws in your state, which have everything to do with your decision. Indeed, for some people this is also their last step. The laws vary greatly from state to state; in some places you must have teaching qualifications, but other states waive that requirement. (It is said to be so difficult to get permission in North Dakota, for example, that parents of some gifted children have already moved just across state lines to reside in more liberal states.) If everything's legal, get in touch with home-schooling advocates in your state. Advocacy groups in Louisiana have been successful in modernizing and liberalizing laws there; consider legislative pressure to remove unnecessarily stringent hurdles to home schooling.

The parents of one profoundly gifted child, whose creative and musical talents were evident from the beginning, were concerned about the goodness of fit with her kindergarten. The child's intellectual abilities far exceeded her emotional maturity, and things got worse as the teacher and system failed to come together for the advancement of the girl's abilities. Their daughter "began to regress," the parents recall. "We felt we couldn't do worse by teaching at home, so we might as well try." Child and parents were very pleased with the results, and their home academy served the girl for three years. They are now home schooling her younger brother. The parents now feel the strongest reason to teach at home is the ability to do what conventional schooling was not doing: building their children's confidence in their ability to direct their own learning. Some formal schooling can discourage creativity.

These parents report that home schooling takes less time than many believe. No standing in line, no bus ride, no waiting for twenty other children to master a point the gifted child caught on first hearing. Much of their curriculum came from life; science and math were often part of helping prepare meals. Their daughter was able to work independently part of the time, conferring frequently with her mother while working on structured projects.

If the thought of home schooling more than one of your children intimidates you, remember that years ago many children attended rural one-room schools where one teacher might have two dozen children of varying ages and abilities. He would determine the levels at which each child was performing and group them according to ability and interest. All the children would work on a single topic at levels appropriate for their development, then regroup to do other work. Like that teacher, you can group all your children for field trips and reading aloud the classics and other stories, with questions geared to each child's level.

Many resources provide further guidance on home schooling. *Better Than School* by Nancy Wallace describes her own experience home schooling two highly gifted children. Education critic and reformer John Holt, author of *How Children Learn* and *Why Children Fail*, also wrote a book called *Teach Your Own*. In addition, his associates publish a bimonthly national newsletter on home schooling, *Growing Without Schooling*. It includes legal information, a parent information-and-support network, and tips for getting started. Send a stamped, self-addressed envelope for information to: Holt Associates, 729 Boylston St., Boston, MA 02116.

Home Education Magazine comes from Home Education Press, P.O. Box 1083, Tonasket, WA 98855. Copublishers Mark and Helen Hegener offer a $10.25 book, *Alternatives in Education, Family Choices in Education*, which considers a number of nonschool routes, including correspondence, cooperatives, and exchanges.

Nancy Plent, 2 Smith St., Farmingdale, NJ 07727, publishes a monthly newsletter for what she calls the Unschoolers Network. Included are book reviews, resources, announcements, ideas, and articles.

Kathi Kearney, director of the Hollingworth Center for *Highly Gifted Children*, Auburn, ME, and editor of Highly Gifted Children, cites these additional helpful sources in her comprehensive roundup of home schooling issues in the January 1989 issue of *Understanding Our Gifted:*

Legal insurance: Home School Legal Defense Association, 731 Walker Rd., Suite E-2, Great Falls, VA 22006.

Updated listings of state laws and legislation in process: Hewitt Research Foundation, P.O. Box 9, Washougal, WA 98671.

Curriculum publishers: Hewitt-Moore Child Development Center (K-12), P.O. Box 9, Washougal, WA 98671; Oak Meadow School (K-8), P.O. Box G, Ojai, CA 93023; Konos Curriculum (K-6), P.O. Box 1534, Richardson, TX 75083.

When you continue to teach your child at home instead of sending him to school, all the resources you used when he was what we call a preschooler—the term seems a misnomer in this context, doesn't it?—continue to be a part of his surroundings. The people with whom he comes into contact, the places he sees as you run to the supermarket, the books he's been reading, continue to serve him, whether he's in a formal school or staying at home.

So does your computer, if you own one. It may provide another avenue of outside sources of enrichment. Your library or local computer- users group may have a bank of public domain software to share or trade. For details, find the appropriate magazine for your brand of computer in the library or on the newsstand. There's no better time to familiarize yourself with the computer as a tool. Periodicals such as Gifted Children Monthly frequently review software for children, and your library's back copies of the computer magazines have periodic features on children's fare.

Whatever you choose for your child—nursery school, preschool, play group, kindergarten, early or late entry, private, parochial, public, or at-home schools—you are from his birth your child's first teacher. With luck you will continue to be one of the people who shapes his life as long as you both live. At each step you are his mentor and advocate. Choose his pathways with an eye to the past, an awareness of the present, and a vision of the future.

7

Testing Intelligence

What a pity that Einstein, Euclid, Leonardo da Vinci, and Newton flourished before the invention of the intelligence quotient. Too bad we'll never know how smart they were, right? Nonetheless, there *were* indications. Probably their mothers knew there was something special about them . . .

Perhaps the biggest paradox in education, in general, and gifted education, in particular, is that, for all the imperfections of the IQ test as it tries to quantify what we know is a fluid process, it is almost always the first thing we reach for when we try to diagnose or describe a child's giftedness.

Using an IQ test to begin to measure the scope of giftedness is like taking the blood pressure of a trauma victim with multiple injuries. Yes, it's part of the picture, and it's among the first things you need to know for any "diagnosis." But by itself it tells you very little about why the victim needs treatment. Your senses perceive other things more difficult to measure but no less apparent to you. Giftedness has many facets that can't be measured by the IQ test, and a number of highly gifted children may deliver genuinely unimpressive results when given IQ tests.

The IQ is a comparative measuring device. As originally devised, it represented the difference between chronological age and something known as "mental age"; an 8-year-old capable of answering questions typically expected of 12-year-olds would have an IQ of 150. The original formula, Mental age over Chronological age times 100, is no longer this simple, because children now are compared only with children their own age. But the concept of mental age is still used informally; it can be derived from IQ and helps in planning what educational materials should be used.

Your child's IQ score may be a useful predictor of his performance in the school years ahead. (It doesn't reliably predict how he'll do in life, however, there being a number of external factors that influence that outcome.) The middle fifty percent of the population have IQs between 90 and 110. Two percent score above 132 on the Stanford-Binet test, and two percent score below 68.

Another comparative look at how the population stacks up:

3 out of 100 have an IQ of 130
1 out of 1,000 have an IQ of 150
1 out of 10,000 have an IQ of 160
1 out of 1,000,000 have an IQ of 180

If you were a school administrator, you might consider yourself effective if you met the needs of ninety percent of the population that had IQ scores between 70 and 130. But what of the top and bottom five to ten percent? To contribute their full potential to the benefit of society, both ends of the spectrum need and deserve special accommodations.

Since its inception the IQ test has been criticized by those who feared it would be used to oppress individuals or social classes or races. Some who concluded that certain races were inherently less intelligent tried to bar the immigration of particular nationalities. Walter Lippman, the influential essayist-columnist, warned that it could be used to oppress or suppress. The Nazis used tests they declared would uncover the best Teutonic intelligence, but the real agenda was the elimination of "certain undesirable elements."

So, from its inception, the IQ test has been something more than a neutral number, an index such as a body temperature of 98.6 degrees Fahrenheit or the Dow-Jones Average. Still, indexes are good to have and enormously useful, whether we're looking at the stock market, our body temperature, or the population of our third grade. But the IQ is only a number. Moses didn't carry it down from a mountaintop etched on tablets. It's subject to a number of criticisms. In 1987 a survey of 661

professionals with expertise in intelligence and aptitude testing elicited
these criticisms:

88 percent complained that IQ tests can't measure creativity
73 percent charged that there's no measure of "adaptation to environment," another criterion determining intelligence
42 percent pointed out that tests don't measure an individual's
capacity to *acquire* knowledge

Other shortcomings listed in responses to this study, the "Survey of
Expert Opinion on Intelligence and Aptitude Test" published in
American Psychologist (February 1987): Factors unrelated to intelligence—nervousness, motivation, the examiner's language or attitude—have the potential to skew test results. Because the language
draws heavily from white, middle-class experience, disadvantaged
young people and nonwhites have long been said to be discriminated
against by the tests. Moreover, some of the questions may no longer be
relevant to some children's experience ("Where does turpentine come
from?" "If snow is white, coal is ————?" Where do kids see coal or
turpentine?).

A number of factors can help children get a higher-than-average score
on individual tests. Here are several Jane M. Healy in *Your Child's
Growing Mind* cites:

- A large fund of practical knowledge and life experiences; older
  children who read widely have an advantage on verbal tests.
- A good vocabulary; they know the meanings of many words and are
  able to formulate good definitions for them.
- The ability to size up a problem quickly.
- A good immediate memory and understanding for oral directions,
  sentences, or a series of numbers.
- The ability to understand and talk about relationships (How are
  things alike? Different?).
- An enjoyment of a challenge, and a willingness to try something that
  looks "hard."
- The ability to risk; a willingness to make a sensible guess.
- Persistence; the ability to try different problem solutions.
- The ability to accept failure and get on with the next problem.

- A lack of impulsivity; the ability to stop and think through a problem and go back and check the results, even under time pressure.

HELP IS COMING

Two eminent researchers are working independently on wholly new instruments and methods for measuring intelligence. Howard Gardner of Harvard University's Graduate School of Education and author of *Frames of Mind* suggests that there are seven broad categories of intelligence. Besides the three conventional ones—verbal, mathematical, and spatial—Gardner lists musical ability, bodily skills, adroitness in dealing with others, and self-knowledge.

"In defense of the label 'intelligence,'" wrote Kevin McKean in "Intelligence: New Ways to Measure the Wisdom of Man," in *Discover* magazine (October 1985)—a special issue on that subject—"Gardner argues that each of the seven abilities can be destroyed by particular brain damage, each shows up in highlighted form in the talents of gifted people or 'idiots savants,' and each involves unique cognitive skills." Gardner opposes any single-number IQ-like scale in representing intelligence.

Psychologist Robert Sternberg of Yale University and author of *Beyond IQ* poses his "triarchic theory" of intelligence, comprising:

- Componential (involving analytical thinking).
- Experiential (involving creative insight).
- Contextual (involving the ability to manipulate the environment to one's best advantage).

"In my opinion," Sternberg writes, "the most critical need in ability testing today is to develop measures that are more sensitive to real-world kinds of intelligence." Of the three aspects of intelligence in his model, an IQ test deals only with the componential.

Regarding giftedness, Sternberg notes that using a one-dimensional scale such as IQ leads to the view that giftedness and retardation are the opposite ends of a single spectrum. But the attributes that distinguish intellectual giftedness are not the same as those that best distinguish retardation. He proposes that a "key psychological basis of intellectual giftedness resides in what might be referred to as 'insight skills.'" Other aspects of giftedness include superior ability to deal with novel tasks and situations in general and adeptness at applying intellectual skills to the task or situation in which they display their gifts.

On IQ tests, Sternberg says,

Applied conservatively and with full respect for all of the available information, tests can be of some use. Misapplied, or overused, they are worse than nothing. We must remember that the fact that a test score is (or appears to be) precise does not mean that it is valid.

And,

The assumption that "smart is fast" permeates our entire society. When we refer to someone as "quick" we are endowing him or her with one of the primary attributes that we perceive an intelligent person to have.

The assumption that more intelligent people are rapid information processors also underlies the overwhelming majority of tests used in identification of the gifted, including creativity as well as intelligence tests . . . I would argue that this assumption is a gross overgeneralization: It is true for some people and for some mental operations, but not for all people or all mental operations. What is critical is not speed *per se* but rather speed selection: knowing when and being able to function rapidly or slowly according to task or situational demands.

Like Gardner, Sternberg is working on an intelligence test that more accurately represents the aspects of his model.

USING IQ TESTS

Given their shortcomings, then, when should parents elect to have an IQ test administered to their preschool child?

First, there may be a need for an independent assessment tool to help make an educational decision. You may feel your child would not benefit from being held back from kindergarten, but his birthday is a week beyond the cutoff point. Would he be better off waiting a year or should you try for an early admission? You might then decide to have him tested for early entrance; when the tester understands your reason, the report should include both the IQ score *and* an evaluation of the psychological climate of testing—would he be frustrated by the materials and situations or does he seem able to handle them? After you see the results you can decide whether to apply. If you do, use the test results only as evidence to support your viewpoint, not as a mandate to the school from an outsider. Offer the school a photocopy of the tester's report only if it is requested. Be persuasive, but respectful.

Parents sometimes choose private testing when they feel the child is being kept out of a gifted program arbitrarily. Here is one family's experience:

> In September our second-grade son was passed over for the school's gifted program. Quite legitimately, they claimed; his group test showed him below the 125 IQ cutoff for the program. We asked a private child psychologist to administer the Wechsler IQ test; his IQ was 147. The school accepted him to the program.
>
> Later his younger sister got to the second grade and we asked why she hadn't been selected for the program. Turns out she was out with flu the day they tested for admission, and they told us there would be no more testing till September of the next year. Off we went to the private psychologist. Same trick: back with the report on her 149 IQ. They accepted *her* to the program.
>
> When her gifted coordinator noticed some deficiency in word attack [breaking down into components, sounding out, placing in context], she suggested a screening by the district psychologist. Same thing, 144 IQ this time. A year later a graduate student who needed volunteers gave her the Stanford-Binet as research for a thesis. This time our daughter's IQ came up 153. Now we had three separate IQ tests and testers, and given the margin for error at that range, we felt they pretty much agreed on her IQ.
>
> That is, until fifth grade in another district. Her achievement test scores were low; she hated school and didn't want to return in the fall. To help us diagnose the situation the school had a workup done by their psychologist, who gave her—what else—an IQ test. Result? 130. We asked how that could be, given consistent results by three different testers. His answer was that they were wrong and he was right . . . she wasn't gifted after all. He seemed quite scornful of her, especially of her failure to locate Peru in South America; she said it was in Africa. In his view, that meant she couldn't possibly be gifted.

Several points come to mind as we hear this family's story. First, IQ tests are set to give accurate positive results and false negatives. That is, if your IQ tests at 140, you might have even superior ability, but not lower. If your intelligence is at age level, your IQ is 100; you can't get a 120 score by fluke or strategy. The same is true of pregnancy tests, by the way; they are determined to allow a false negative but never a false positive.

Second, the margin of error on scores increases proportionately with the distance above or below 100. Elizabeth Hagen, co-developer of the Stanford-Binet Intelligence Scale, Revision IV, explains in *Roeper Review*, February 1986:

> For most widely used tests, the standard error of measurement is larger for high scores than for average scores because the number of items on which higher scores are based is fewer than the number of items on which average scores are based. At the upper levels of the score distribution a difference of two items correct can change a score markedly, whereas a change of this size in the middle of the distribution will have little or no effect on the obtained standard score.

Third, group intelligence tests, while they're inexpensive to administer and don't have to be given by trained psychologists, are far less reliable than individual tests. If your child scores 120 in the group screening, she could possibly come in at 140 on an individual test, according to a study of junior high school students. That's why most experts recommend against excluding a child from a program because of an arbitrary threshold. Barbara Clark suggests using a cutoff no higher than 115 if group screening must be used to inventory the talent pool for a program; even with that level you'll exclude eight percent of the children who could perform at a 135 IQ level on individual tests. According to C. Pegnato and J. Birch in "Locating Gifted Children in Junior High Schools: A Comparison of Methods," published in *Exceptional Children* (1959), if, on the other hand, the school considers only students whose group tests score at 120 or above, they would unfairly eliminate 20 percent of students capable of 136 or higher scores on individual tests.

A number of factors may influence the answers of gifted children who take group intelligence tests. For example, the advanced child may hurry ahead and miss details of the questions, then tire of waiting for the prescribed time to move to new sections. The creative child might examine all aspects of multiple-choice questions, overlooking the obvious answers and using all the time allotted, while the perfectionist might go back over his answers, reconsider, and rationalize changing correct answers to incorrect ones.

IQ TESTS AS SCREENING DEVICES

Psychologists and gifted-education consultants Sheila C. Perino and Joseph Perino in their book, *Parenting the Gifted: Developing the Promise,* caution that

> group IQ tests are helpful as a coarse screening technique when (1) the bottom cutoff (lowest acceptable) group score is kept liberal; (2) individual exceptions to the cutoff group are evaluated on a case-by-case basis; and (3) all children receive an individual test prior to entrance into the program.

According to Jane Healy of Cleveland State University in her book *Your Child's Growing Mind*:

> Parents should never authorize any important educational decision about a child on the basis of group IQ tests. An individual battery gives a fuller and more accurate picture, but still should be considered only as a part of a full appraisal of ability.

Most intelligence tests comprise several subtests of particular abilities. Many experts feel that each of these scores should be taken individually instead of being combined into one score. In this way, strengths and weaknesses are pinpointed with greater clarity. Moreover, two children may arrive at the same overall IQ score with two very different profiles. Different subscores call for different kinds of instruction to maximize the children's potential. A school district that touts a gifted program but puts students with different types of giftedness in one accelerated math program, or a single reading program, is missing the point. Just as a carpenter takes more than one tool to the work site, the school must use a combination of instruments to place children in a gifted program.

Barbara Clark suggests, in *Growing Up Gifted*, a number of entrance qualifiers, including:

* Nomination forms—from teachers, principal, counselor, psychologist, and others
* Teacher reports of student functioning—including intellectual, physical, social, and emotional functioning; learning style and motivation

- Family history and student background—provided by parents—including historical and developmental data on the student, health and medical records of student and family, educational and occupational background of parents, description of family unit, anecdotes of the student in the home that indicate unusual capacity and early development, family activities and interests, and the child's out-of-school activities and interests
- Peer identification
- Student inventory—of self, values, interests, and attitudes toward school and out-of-school activities
- Student work and achievements
- Multidimensional screen tests

David Elkind, author of *The Hurried Child* and outspoken opponent of premature acceleration, cautions in his article "Superbaby Syndrome Can Lead to Elementary School Burnout," published in the journal *Young Children* (March 1987) that

> the best measure of children's adjustment and learning is obtained through careful observation by skilled observers who know the child well, preferably teachers and parents. No decision about a child's appropriate placement in school should be made on the basis of a single test score.

The process at work in Howard Gardner's Harvard research, mentioned at the beginning of this chapter, is encouraging and promising. Here are highlights of the description by researcher Carey Wexler-Sherman to the National Association for the Education of Young Children at their Washington, D.C., convention in 1986, quoted in *Growing Child Research Review* (June 1987):

> Intelligence is no longer defined as a single static entity that can be captured numerically. We now have broader, more comprehensive views of intelligence. Assessment should not be a process in isolation, but a process in context. When assessment extends over the entire term, we capture evolution as well as refinement.
> As Project Spectrum children go about the daily business of preschool life, they encounter special, enriched, low-tech materials—many in the

form of appealing games—as part of the curriculum. There are no timed tests with "correct" answers, no unfamiliar settings or unfamiliar adults.

The teacher directly observes the children, keeps a precise, up-to-date observational checklist, and works closely with the parents, who are regarded as a key source of information. "Kids bring different parts of themselves to different settings. A child's working style, in particular, can differ from home to school."

The teacher not only presents the assessment tasks but must interpret the information the tasks provide, using descriptive, jargon-free English that will be understandable to parents as well as other educators who will receive the child's portfolio. The information should give all adults concerned more handles to use in helping the child and enable them to make informed, sensitive choices concerning each youngster.

Until such careful procedures are more common, Barbara Clark urges those of us on the home front not to lose hope. "At present," she cautions in *Growing Up Gifted,*

there are few early learning programs available that provide well-rounded, integrated, and enriched programs; there are even fewer that provide appropriately for young gifted children. With this in mind I would be more concerned about challenging all children from where they are, allowing continuous progress and enriching experiences, and letting the children guide us to their next steps than I would be about formal identification. Appropriate, stimulating experiences are our best way to nurture giftedness.

An appropriate method for dealing with all children seems to be the Renzulli Revolving Door model. (See Sally M. Reis and Joseph S. Renzulli, "A Case for a Broadened Conception of Giftedness," in *Phi Delta Kappan* [May 1982].) Given the imprecision of tests, Renzulli's model, proposed in 1981, advocates flexible procedures to identify a "talent pool" of twenty percent of the school population. Classroom teachers scheduled enrichment activities

to capitalize on existing interests, promote new and diversified interests, and to develop a wide variety of thinking processes and research skills. A procedure called "curriculum compacting" helped them to cover regular curricular materials at speeds commensurate with their varying ability level. Individualizing the regular curriculum in this fashion allowed fast learners to "buy" time for accelerated learning activities or enrichment experiences.

Action information—dynamic interactions that take place when a student becomes inspired by a particular topic, issue, event, or form of creative expression—triggered a new level of involvement: "These youngsters were allowed to pursue their interest under the direction of a resource teacher for a given period of time. They continued to go to a resource room until they had completed their projects."

Entrants in the Renzulli program were both the identified top five percent on standardized tests for intelligence or achievement, *as well as* a group whose abilities were well above average but not enough to put them in the top five percent. But groups participated equally in all aspects of the program, and in data analysis afterward both groups showed equal benefit, *provided the students showed both creativity and task commitment.* Teachers were overwhelmingly in favor of the Revolving Door entrance over traditional test scores.

The key of the Renzulli program may be its discovery that far more than the top five percent of the student population can benefit from enrichment, acceleration, flexibility, and interest grouping for projects. Surely the revolving door is less vulnerable to charges of elitism and less likely to omit eligible students.

One school psychologist told us of channeling a third-grade girl away from her district's gifted program, which dealt with reading, math, and science. Parents had nominated the girl, who had some learning disabilities but clearly excelled at reading comprehension. The psychologist determined that the girl was indeed verbally gifted but was just holding her own in other courses, and not likely to develop the fluency and facility needed to keep up in the high-tech program. Fearing the other students' rapid pace would make the girl feel inferior, she found against the girl's admission to the program. Her motivation was the girl's self-concept. The Renzulli plan would avoid her having to make choices of this kind.

Not that we should throw out individual testing in the interim and wait for Gardner, Sternberg, and others to further revolutionize our thinking. We can't afford to do nothing; as the educator says, every year, all new kids. By the time tests being developed today are standardized, you might be attending graduation exercises (and maybe they'll be your grandchildren's!). So in the meantime all we can do is make sure that the current tests are used properly and in context.

Linda Silverman in her article "The IQ Controversy: Conceptions and Misconceptions," published in the *Roeper Review* (February 1986) emphasizes that testing can identify some candidates for inclusion in gifted programs; but when an otherwise qualified child isn't accepted, it's up to us to take over where testing leaves off. A low score shouldn't keep a child who shows other signs of giftedness from a program, Silverman continues, if he can demonstrate giftedness by some other means.

The usefulness of a test in identifying giftedness depends on how you define giftedness and what age level you're working with. When children are younger, the differential in their development is much greater and easier to identify with tests, Silverman explains. By the time they are in junior high school "generalized abilities are channeled into specific domains, and aptitude tests are considered better indicators of ability than intelligence tests."

When the purpose of testing is to gain entrance to a special gifted program, the *nature* of the program has to be kept in mind. If the program's emphasis is on creativity, music, art, and the like, methods other than IQ scores should be used to find candidates.

INDIVIDUAL TEST INSTRUMENTS

The most common group tests for measuring IQ as noted by Sheila and Joseph Perino in *Parenting the Gifted: Developing the Promise*, are:

Preschool to Kindergarten:

1. Goodenough-Harris Drawing Test. A drawing of a person is performed by the child. Points are obtained for the accuracy of the figure. Fine motor deficits will not necessarily depress the score.
2. Vane Kindergarten Test. This test has three parts: a figure drawing scored similarly to the Goodenough, a vocabulary portion, and a section in which geometric shapes must be reproduced.

Kindergarten to Twelfth Grade

1. California Test of Mental Maturity. This test has five factors, dealing with memory, language, reasoning, and perceptual and mathematical ability.
2. Lorge-Thorndike Intelligence Tests. The kindergarten and first-grade parts are nonverbal. The other grade levels have both verbal and nonverbal sections. Skills tested include vocabulary, classification, and relationships between words or symbols.
3. Otis-Lennon Mental Ability Test and Kuhlmann-Anderson Intelligence Tests. These tests are similar to the foregoing measures.

Besides the group tests, your district or your private psychologist may use one or more of the intelligence tests now currently in favor. Since you may find yourself in meetings in which the scores are tossed about like tennis balls, it might be helpful to be conversant with the tests. Knowing the lingo might give you equal footing in a meeting in which you're already outnumbered eight-to-one by school personnel.

After you learn what instruments your district is using to evaluate your child, one place to read more about them is the *Buros Mental Measurements Yearbook*, an exhaustive compilation of studies of various test instruments by test psychologists and other professionals. When a new test or edition is released, reviews of it appear a few years later. You can find ammunition for or against the use of most instruments if you have time to read some scholarly prose. The *BMMY* is produced by the University of Nebraska; at this writing the ninth version, released in 1985, is in most libraries.

One psychologist in private practice reminded us that some school system psychologists may exaggerate a bright child's high score in the context of the examiner's day-to-day experience, which usually consists of administering assessments of slow learners or students who are having problems simply trying to get up to grade level.

Here are some of the instruments you may encounter:

1. Wechsler Preschool and Primary Scale of Intelligence (called WIP-PSI).
    Used for 3- to 6-year-olds.

Verbal section: information, vocabulary, arithmetic, similarities, comprehension, and sentences.

Performance section: animal house, picture completion, mazes, geometric design and block design.

Takes about an hour to administer.

Not as useful for gifted children because of its low ceiling; gifted preschoolers who perform above the 6 1/2-year-level top off the scale. If this instrument is used alone on your 5-year-old who is capable of doing 8-year-old work, this test will rate him only 6.5+.

2. Wechsler Intelligence Scale for Children—Revised 1974 (called WISC-R).

Ages 6 to 16.

Most recommended test for gifted children over age 6.

Geared to more specific age range than Stanford-Binet; verbal and performance breakdown are said to give better overall picture of child's ability.

Verbal section: information, similarities, arithmetic, vocabulary, comprehension, and digit span (mostly untimed).

Performance section: picture completion, picture arrangement, block design, object assembly, coding, mazes (timed).

Takes about an hour to administer.

Yield: three scores: verbal, performance, and full scale.

3. Stanford-Binet.

Ages 2 to Adult.

Results in single mental age and IQ score.

Takes about an hour to administer.

Heavy emphasis on language skills.

Most frequently recommended test for preschool gifted; (ceiling higher than WIPPSI) and most preferred by psychologists. The recent revised optional version sometimes runs long; some testers wonder if it is cost-effective with gifted children, who may take in excess of two hours to complete the battery.

The answer manual is not particularly forgiving of divergent thinkers. Unless the answer is worded pretty nearly as called for, the examiner could disallow it. A divergent but contextually correct answer might be more complete than called for by the test. Much depends on the experience and skill of the examiner, who should be carefully chosen. When having a preschool age child tested be sure to choose a tester who has had experience working with that age group.

Both the WISC-R and Stanford-Binet have a ceiling of 160 IQ, so higher scores must be estimated. Both are felt to be disadvantageous to culturally divergent groups.

4.   McCarthy Scales of Children's Abilities.

Ages 2 1/2 to 8.

Takes one hour.

To receive a high score, the subject must score high on all subtests. This is a disadvantage for those whose gifts are not evenly distributed.

5.   Kaufman Assessment Battery for Children (called K-ABC).

Ages 2 1/2 to 12 1/2.

Three intelligence scales:

Sequential processing.

Simultaneous processing.

Mental processing composite.

Introduced in 1983.

"These intelligence scales focus on process [how children solve problems] rather than content . . . and intentionally deemphasize acquired factual knowledge and applied school-related skills such as arithmetic," claims its constructor, Alan S. Kaufman.

Includes an achievement scale, too, composed of measures of general information, language concepts, arithmetic, letter reading and word reading and reading comprehension.

Alan and Nadeen L. Kaufman, constructors of the test, suggest it is especially useful with gifted children; but this has not been proven empirically in the field. It doesn't seem to measure what children have picked up from the environment. "May measure some internal learning ability, but whether the child can apply that really isn't demonstrated on the Kaufman, from what I can tell," reported one psychologist, Richard Aronoff, who regularly screens applicants for a Chicago-area private school for gifted students.

Here are some quick screening tests:

1.   Peabody Picture Vocabulary Test.

Ages 2 1/2 to 18 years.

Takes 10 to 15 minutes.

Nonverbal test of receptive vocabulary—understanding what is heard.

"This type of test appraises only one type of cognitive skill—word knowledge; it does not tap problem-solving or reasoning skills, which are extremely important predictors of outstanding achievement . . . such a narrowly focused test should not be used in an identification program for the gifted," according to Elizabeth Hagen, in *Identification of the Gifted.*

"The Peabody is not able to distinguish the gifted child. Scores tend to cluster around the average range even for intellectually gifted children," according to Suzanne McFarland in "Guidelines for the Identification of Young Gifted and Talented Children," published in *The Young Gifted Child.*

2.   Slosson Intelligence Test (1963).

Ages infancy to adult.

Takes 20 minutes.

Suffers from limited coverage of cognitive abilities; should not be used to identify or exclude the gifted.

3.   Raven Progressive Matrices (1956).

Ages 5 1/2 and up.

Nonverbal reasoning; colored designs with a piece missing; subject must choose piece that fits. Recent standardizing allows for more accurate interpretation of scores. Since the test is nonverbal, it gives no indication of how information and knowledge are picked up from the environment, nor whether the child has good language skills.

Works well, however, for language-delayed or non-English-speaking children.

The following are the most common achievement tests administered:

1.   Metropolitan Readiness Test, Level 1.

Assesses preschoolers' kindergarten readiness with seven sub-tests: auditory memory, rhyming, letter recognition, visual matching, school language and listening, qualitative language, copying.

2.   Stanford Early School Achievement Test.

For kindergartners and first graders, deals with mathematics, environment, letters and sounds, aural comprehension.

3.   Test of Basic Experiences, Level K.

Tests the child's concept mastery; related to early academic achievement.

4.   Peabody Individual Achievement Test (PIAT).

Tests spelling, math, reading comprehension, and general knowledge. One study with intellectually advantaged children indicates a high correlation between the results of the Peabody Individual Achievement Test (PIAT) and other standardized tests. The PIAT measures academic skills reliably among this group.

Useful as comprehensive screening instruments are, they tend to concentrate on a single aspect of intelligence. If you are strong in the component they test, you come out looking good; but when tested on your weakest point you could look like a dunce. Almost no one seeks a career in his area of least expertise. If your child's educational program is ever decided by a single instrument, you should be aware of that instrument and its strengths and weaknesses.

Creativity tests are also subject to misleading results. The data they yield really have to be viewed in context with other information if they are going be useful.

The following instruments are used to measure creativity:

1. Divergent thinking tests—scored for ideational fluency and originality

    Many of the most commonly used tests for creativity were framed by E. Paul Torrance.

    A. Thinking Creatively With Pictures.

    For ages 5 though adult.

    Is especially appropriate for children who have well-developed fine motor skills, since it involves drawing and representing symbols. A child who could imagine the symbols but couldn't draw them with precision might test low.

    B. Thinking Creatively in Action and Movement (Torrance).

    For 3- to 8-year-olds.

    For example, in one part, the subject is asked to move about the room in as many different ways as possible; the broader the range and variety of locomotions, the higher the score. Original modes, such as walking backwards on one's knees, are scored higher than the most common responses—crawling or pretending to drive or fly.

    C. Thinking Creatively with Sounds and Music (by Torrance, Khatena, and Cunnington).

    For ages 8 and up.

In one phase recorded sounds are played and the subject is asked to identify them. The more the answers go beyond the practiced, commonplace, or habitual, the higher the score.

D. Creativity Assessment Packet (CAP) by Dr. Frank Williams.

Consists of tests of divergent thinking and feeling and an observational scale (see below). Subjects are given printed sheets with various shapes partially drawn in twelve squares; they are asked to complete the pictures by drawing whatever the shapes suggest to them. Evaluations consider flexibility and fluency, originality, elaboration, and imaginative titles.

Other instruments commonly used include Guilford tests, Wallach & Kogan tests, and Getzels & Jackson tests.

2. Inventories that assess personality and biographical traits:

A. Preschool and Primary Interest Descriptor (PRIDE).

A preschool and kindergarten parent inventory of fifty questions to help identify relative position in four dimensions: Many Interests, Independence-Perseverance, Imagination-Playfulness, and Originality. High-scorers are identified as showing high interest in learning, stories, books and things around them; preferring to play alone and persevere with difficult tasks; enjoying make-believe humor; having unusual ideas and asking unusual questions. Low-scorers show less curiosity, have fewer interests, prefer easier tasks, follow the lead of other children, and tend to be more serious and realistic.

B. The Williams Scale.

A Teacher-Parent Observational Scale, presents behavioral factors (Fluent, Flexible, Original, Elaborative Thinker; Curious and Inquisitive, Imaginative, Complex, and Courageous risk-taking student) and lists six evidences of each. Yields a 100-point index of comparative creativity. Part of the Williams Creativity Assessment Packet (see above).

C. Group Inventory for Finding Talent (GIFT).

Consists of yes/no items in lower-, middle-, and upper-elementary school forms. The test was developed in 1975, revised in 1980, and had dimensional scores scaled in 1982 for factors like Imagination, Independence, and Many Interests. Subjects are scored higher for having interest in "art, writing, and learning about life long ago and in other countries." Subjects who earn high scores for independence "enjoy aloneness; they prefer challenge, are not afraid to be different from their peers." Those who score high in Imagination "are curious, enjoy questioning, make-believe and humor; low scorers are more literal and realistic and less curious."

Interesting caveats are imprinted on the GIFT test results form. According to Sylvia Rimm in "The Characteristics Approach: Identification and Beyond," published in *Gifted Child Quarterly* (Fall 1984): "High scores (85–99 percentile) indicate that the child has characteristics similar to those which are typical of highly creative children. Characteristics measured by this inventory include interest range, independence, perseverance, flexibility, curiosity, and biographical information. Low or average scores do not indicate that a child is necessarily not creative. The inventory was not designed to screen children out of gifted programs."

Rimm emphasizes that creativity tests should not be used to eliminate candidates from gifted programs, but rather "to help find children who have creative characteristics and who are not already identified for the gifted program. . . . If society claims to value creativity, then gifted programming must be beyond providing academic challenge. Schools must combine our understanding of creative process, creative attitudes, and creative characteristics with the acquisition of information synergistically so that gifted programming can complement the acquisition of knowledge with creative thinking."

Whatever our reason to use a test, we need to remember as St. Paul wrote that "for now we see through a glass, darkly." We use tests not to see the entire panorama. We can never expect to see everything, because some of what's there is not wholly perceivable.

8

Who's in Charge Here?

Whose responsibility is it to make sure that children get a complete, effective, enabling education?

The Board of Education?
The PTA?
The state education director?
The U.S. Department of Education?
The parents?

If you answered all of the above, you're partly right.

Hundreds of years ago, education was for the privileged few, who were often quite enlightened, even by today's standards. But progress brought reformation and a number of inalienable rights, among them the promise of state-supported public schooling for all. The progress across the board has been enormous, but along the way we forfeited some of our ability to enable the exceptionally fast learner to move ahead at his own pace and in pursuit of his own goals.

Quite simply, the American Way of Education works for the great majority of its customers, the average children for whom it is set up. It is less suited to the minorities: the physically handicapped, the emotionally unstable, the slow learner, the culturally disadvantaged, the non-English-speaking, and the gifted. In the last several years, many of these groups have formed a vocal lobby and have forced schools to provide full service and individualized attention, with accommodations in curricula, programs, and facilities. However, advocacy for the gifted has been slower to take hold. There *are* national organizations for the gifted and even federal guidelines, standards, and funding. Still, the biggest single influence on individuation in your child's school is quite often you.

Moreover, the years from ages 4 to 7 are intensely critical to the maintenance of your child's potential giftedness, which is a process responsive to cultivation and vulnerable to neglect and destruction. A number of studies have demonstrated the frailty of potential giftedness, especially in the preschool and kindergarten period. Witness:

- Intellectually advanced children do not develop equally well under all circumstances. (This is especially true of the extraordinarily gifted.) Early identification and special programming are important, according to Leta Hollingworth and Harold McCurdy.
- Research discussed in *Young Children* (November 1987) indicates that early childhood educators are notoriously poor at spotting gifted children.
- There is evidence noted by Ann Sutherland and Marcel L. Goldschmid to suggest that truly superior children who are perceived by their teacher to have only average intelligence decline in intelligence achievement-test performance relative to equally superior children whose abilities are recognized by their teachers.
- Gifted first-grade students placed in special programs gained an average of two academic years during a single nine-month period, while gifted children in regular classes gained only the usual one year, according to a study by Ruth A. Martinson.

Because very few districts even think about looking for giftedness before the fourth grade, the initiative until then will have to come from you. In chapter 6 we discussed the choice of kindergarten and primary school programs. Now we address the role a parent plays in ensuring maximum encouragement by the school you've chosen. Since there is strength in numbers it may be helpful to enlist other parents in your movement.

We see three kinds of advocacy as you and your child enter the world of organized education: *prevention, intervention,* and *convention.* Prevention gets education off to the right start and heads off problems before they arise. Intervention keeps education on course, and convention crystallizes community interests to ensure that the needs of gifted children in your schools are met long after your children have been graduated.

PREVENTION

To get through your children's school years with the fewest hurt feelings, misunderstandings, and confrontations, try to anticipate problems and catch them early.

Probably a great many difficulties throughout our lives could be avoided if we had better lines of communication with those around us. School is just one of the places where that's true, and the year looks endless when you're not getting along, especially if you have another child or two coming up through the ranks. Better to work with the school staff, then, and establish yourself as their partner in bringing out the best in your child. To many people that seems like second nature—it's what they do naturally. Others don't know what to do and unknowingly make the wrong impression.

What's the best way to go about being on good terms with your children's teachers?

One: Be a joiner and volunteer in your school system. Join the parent-teacher organization. Volunteer to help in school—in the classroom, on field trips, at registration, and as a resource, sharing stories about your travels or your interests. Sew costumes for the pageant; ride the bus to the zoo; make a treat for the Valentine's Day party; sell sweatshirts to raise money for the new VCR. It's no secret that a friendly face gets a better reception when it's time to deal with a request or a problem. Don't miss the open houses; they're dialogue the school wants you to share.

Two: Give information about your child's personality type and skills and talents when it's time to move on to the next grade or school. Given a chance, school personnel would like to make productive matches of students and teachers, but unless they are informed of who's who they don't always have enough information to avoid mismatches. Many forward-thinking schools ask parents about their child's strengths and weaknesses. It's easier by far to give information that influences teacher assignment than to get your child reassigned after school is in progress.

INTERVENTION

Sooner or later, something might come up at school that needs attention and possibly intervention.

Consider these testimonies from parents we have spoken with—none are literary inventions:

> In third grade his public school teacher threw up her hands and told him she quit; he knew more about her subject than she could ever teach. She told him to keep quiet and stay out of trouble for the balance of the school year. He helped her out by grading papers. He's in a private school now, and thriving.

> Our five-year-old was reading-ready, although she learned on her own. We asked when early reading materials would appear. None were planned. We got a meeting with the principal and the district reading consultant. They told us very patiently that five-year-olds couldn't read. By January the kindergarten teacher was having her distribute papers and artwork—because she could read the names of all her classmates.
> The same kindergarten teacher passed out mazes, but our daughter refused to do them. Why? Teacher held them up and showed the class the proper route through the maze so they could follow it with their pencils. Our daughter wanted to figure it out for herself. We asked the teacher why she showed the kids the answers; she said she didn't want anyone to be frustrated by going into a dead end. We felt we were the ones in the dead end. We moved.

> The mother of a profoundly gifted kindergartner asked for a meeting with the principal and teacher to discuss providing the appropriate advanced curriculum. No way, they said, until her "emotional problem" was solved—that is, her tendency to dissolve into tears when she was frustrated (which was pretty often in this setting). Teacher and principal sent her to the school psychologist, which made the girl even more distant from her classmates. Her reading performance slipped; her mother felt the classmates were less than cordial. Finally her learning was regressing. The year ended with a whimper, and the next year her mother schooled her at home.

How do you know when things aren't fine in *your* child's class? Sometimes you'll hear all the gory details, and then some. Other times, though, you won't get a full picture of what's going on from your child. She'll give you a very one-sided picture of the story or nothing at all.

When problems come up she may want to avoid them, or may not know how to verbalize them. Watch for danger signals of stressful situations.

Jacqulyn Saunders and Pamela Espeland in *Bringing Out the Best* list some of the behavioral signs that may indicate stress somewhere in the child's life. Check further if you observe:

- Any change in sleeping patterns, including wakefulness, bad dreams, or a desire to sleep all the time.
- Any change in eating habits.
- Any change in toilet habits, perhaps coupled with reversion to baby behaviors long outgrown.
- "Perfect" behavior at school but wildly erratic behavior at home; some children store frustration all day and let loose in the acceptance and safety of home.
- Pronounced avoidance behavior—often evidenced by complaints of non-specific ailments.
- General crankiness, weepiness, or diminished ability to roll with the punches.
- The child frequently describes himself in negative terms.
- Total lack of interest in a previously favored activity, not just a shift in interest.

Doubtless there are other symptoms, perhaps as many as there are children in school. Only you will know what changes take place in your child's behavior. Once the root cause is identified, you've got something you can work with.

When a problem does arise, conventional wisdom seems to be to go up the chain of command. First see the teacher, and in a friendly and noncombative way let him know you realize there's some tension in the teacher-child relationship and you'd like his opinion.

Pay attention to body language, eye contact, and other nonverbal signs. Avoid incendiary words; get his side before you negotiate. Be a partner, not an adversary. Both of you ostensibly want the best for your child. Together you should be able to forge a compromise; agree to try it; meet to reassess.

When you deal with teachers, remember that schools can only partially accommodate the gifted student. What our advocacy seeks is a better fit, more individualization. Further accommodation will come from home and family. Approach the school from the stance of seeking to share information; you need to know what the teacher perceives, concludes, recommends, and plans, and you should be willing to offer any observations that may contribute.

Understand the teacher's feelings; respect him even when you disagree; what you offer might make his job easier. Begin your discussions on a common ground. Check periodically to see if the teacher's perceptions match your own. Don't threaten, attack credentials, or point out the painfully obvious. Quote others' observations or other substantiated facts, not just your own views. Ask the teacher's plans; suggest alternatives but don't insist; then wait for results. Enlist other professionals within the system to substantiate (or mediate).

One couple attended midterm parents' night at a supplemental language program and remarked to the teacher that their children didn't seem to be progressing; the children didn't appear to have homework from week to week and they never talked about what the class was doing. The teacher seemed relieved that the parents had inquired. According to her the children hadn't been preparing their homework and in class were unruly and disruptive. Questioned later, the children, one of whom had taken French lessons before, said the rest of the class were beginners and took forever to catch on to the basics. So some modification resulted, and with teamwork the classes improved for all the players. If the parents hadn't spoken up, a difficult situation might have gone uncorrected much longer. Once again, our advice is to go in with questions rather than war clubs.

We asked a seasoned principal, known for his rapport with the parents of his students, what kind of action was most likely to be effective for all parties. Here is his recommendation:

If your contact with the teacher isn't working, ask for an appointment to see the principal. If the principal has been around for more than two weeks, yours won't be the first such request she has received. This may be the first time *you've* had this problem, but it probably isn't the first time she has heard of it. Possibly she already has the basis of a solution in mind.

When you present your case to the principal, have specific examples or evidence with you. If there's a conflict, explain how it makes your child feel. Remember, you're giving hearsay evidence as described by a partisan, your child. The teacher is a firsthand witness and may have a different account. Present the facts as you know them and be willing to listen.

Ask to see some kind of specific improvement within thirty days. If you see it sooner, make a quick call to let the principal know that the progress is encouraging.

After the trial period, schedule another meeting to follow up. If there is no improvement or if the progress isn't satisfactory and you start meeting stone walls, it's time to see the superintendent. But don't threaten. Allow the principal a chance to redouble efforts for another period before going upstairs.

> *Case study:* a father came to the principal to report that his son seemed to have difficulty learning information from print media. Was there any way to introduce curriculum in other media? A meeting was called for the Learning Disability specialist, the child's classroom teacher, the principal, and the learning center director. After discussion they agreed to involve the child in his own independent study, beginning in his area of interest— nature. They let him use the learning center VCR and borrowed all the videos they could get their hands on—nature specials, National Geographic specials, material from their own homes. The boy made notes and reported highlights of his independent study to his classmates. He wrote original stories and reports on the learning center's computer/word processor. Result: one well-served student. One father had acted as his son's advocate in an effective manner.

If you can only remember one rule, says this principal, make it the Golden Rule. "If someone pushes me, I tend to want to push back. If someone yells at me, I want to yell back. If someone is nice to me, I tend to want to be nice."

Here is what most people agree won't work: demands; threats; unsubstantiated claims; yelling; telling professionals what their job should be and how to do it; attacking professional competency.

Here is what often works: fact-finding; compliments; compromise; expressions of confidence; sharing of information that may enlighten the other person and/or make his job easier.

If you are making a case that your child is potentially gifted, bring any evidence you can muster. Comments from other teachers, parent observation checklists from this book or others, and by all means *photocopies* of any diaries or logs that you've kept. Remember that anything you leave behind may be kept in your child's permanent record and sent with him from school to school. Remember your legal right to examine these records from time to time and challenge their veracity or conclusions if you wish.

On the subject of language, James Delisle, who compiled *Gifted Children Speak Out* and coauthored *The Gifted Kids' Survival Guide II*, offers some examples of how to phrase your exchanges (and how *not* to) in seeking admission to a gifted program:

Not "Does this school have a gifted program?" but rather, "How do you address the needs of gifted students in your school?"

Not "Why was my child not placed in your gifted program? He was in one in the last school," but rather "What procedures are in place for students who, in previous schools, were involved in special programs?"

Not "Why is the gifted program limited to one day per week," but rather, "What modifications are made in regular classes for students involved once per week in the gifted program?"

Not "Why isn't there a program until grade 4?" but rather, "What plans do you have for expanding the program to more grades, and what suggestions do you have for us that will help our child right now?"

Not "Wouldn't it make more sense for me to enroll my child in a private school for gifted children," but rather, "What specific programs do you offer that benefit gifted students?"

When a classroom situation appears to be harmful in some way to your child, take stock. If it is actually harmful to his self-esteem or his feelings about school, it is time to intervene. As you analyze the situation, you'll be looking for ways to disarm or defuse it. Quite possibly you can be instrumental in removing tensions, relieving frustrations, coordinating, communicating. If the problem is, say, that a kindergarten teacher can't spot the gifted trees in her overpopulated forest, you and other parents could volunteer to be assistants, either providing the enrichment the gifted population needs or freeing the teacher from some other task and thus allowing her to devote more attention to individuals. You can be aware of behavior common among gifted children; talk with your child, look for a creative solution to problems like boredom. Watch for supplementation opportunities in after-school hours and weekends to fill the gaps.

One third-grader was uncomfortable because her teacher accused her of daydreaming during his instruction periods. She confided to her mother that while his instructions were clear to her on the first run-through, he felt it necessary to repeat and elaborate them for her classmates. She couldn't keep her mind from wandering after she had received, processed, and logged the message.

Clearly it was time for some creative thinking. After a period of analysis, problem identification, brainstorming, and innovative thinking, the girl and her mother came up with a solution. When the teacher gave instructions, the child would analyze his speech and keep a running total of the words he used most frequently. To the teacher it seemed she was unswervingly attentive, and in fact she was. Her secondary goal, the word count, made concentrating on the teacher's words fun. Everybody won!

As she continues through the upper grades, there will be other situations that need innovative solutions. Your children can come up with their own. Urge them to keep the principles of divergent thinking in mind as they look for solutions. Gifted kids can be visionaries. With our encouragement they can find their own solutions.

Meanwhile, the day may come, for a variety of reasons, when there will be a problem that far exceeds your individual ability to sway the school system. Something global will come up and it will be time to mobilize the forces of your neighbors who also parent gifted children. Then it's time to get organized.

CONVENTION: STARTING A PARENTS' GROUP

If you want your district to begin a gifted program or a more comprehensive program, it's time to organize. Substantial progress and successful programs are almost never the product of single-handed advocacy. One extremely vocal parent with a bright kid might be considered a pain in the neck. Sixty vocal parents with forty bright kids are a substantial minority interest group within the school population.

For the moment we'll deal with starting from scratch in a school that doesn't have a gifted program at all. Your first step is to find out how many people support your position. Even if you're new in town, kids usually have a feel for which of their classmates have similar abilities. Or a sympathetic teacher might put you in touch with other families. When you have a committed core of two or three parents, schedule an exploratory meeting. Invite teachers, administrators, school board members, and others who may have a stake in the issue, as well as parents. Build the meeting around a program topic of some sort—an author, a gifted-program coordinator from a nearby university, a parents' organization leader from a nearby town, a child psychologist who has broad experience with gifted children. Publicize your meeting in local papers, PTA or school parent flyers, call-in radio talk shows, church bulletins, wherever you can reach parents. If possible, schedule your speaker on a local radio talk show a week before your meeting. Always include a phone number so parents can call for more information. Try to find out about the people who call. Do their schools meet their needs? What more is needed? Which teachers seem to enjoy and work well with gifted children? Call all the people you can and invite them personally; ask each one to name other parents of gifted children. Get every name and phone number you can, since they will be your power base, whether or not they attend the meeting.

At your initial meeting, pass around a sign-up sheet so you can follow up with materials and news. Find out who's interested in proceeding with a plan for a program and select a steering committee. Ask for information about needs—any problems, inadequacies, or deficits that can be addressed, short term or long term. (Keep your feet on the ground; you can't rebuild the school program over the weekend.) The steering committee will meet to assess the needs in your school, draft a plan, form bylaws, and discuss a budget if necessary. This group can also set a program for the second meeting. Try to identify parents who will help with programs, newsletters, communications, or any other need.

If you can manage it, a newsletter is the best way of keeping everybody informed of your progress, keeping the idea alive until you can meet again. Include your next meeting and program; local resources; recommended books; updates on gifted classes and activities; names and addresses of school and committee contact people; and anything on appropriate legislation.

Because nothing happens overnight, especially in education, it's smart to recruit parents of new students coming into kindergarten or moving into the neighborhood. It may take you three years to get things running smoothly with the schools. In that time more than half the student population may have matriculated to the next school or moved out of the district. The work you do should live long after you, and unless there's continuity in new families, your labors might disappear the year after you do. Some programs that you start to meet your own children's needs may not be in place until your kids are too old to benefit from them, but your children will always benefit from knowing that you cared enough about their needs to have tried.

The Serving Emotional Needs of the Gifted program at Wright State University suggests $10 per family per year as dues to pay for printing, postage, and incidentals. They say you can expect about half your power base to attend and pay dues about half the time; the committed core will be about one-quarter of the eligible parents. This core can be counted on to steer, pay, lead, and attend. The remaining three-quarters are transient—moving in and out, coming for special programs, but not necessarily following every step of the way. Recommendations: involve fathers in all aspects of programs and committees; involve students in about half your programs; seek funding from the community; become recognized as a credible resource on the gifted in your district; engage in community service activities.

Contact national and state organizations for gifted parents; they can help with guidance and information at several levels along the way, and they will have current information on other groups in your state.

The Gifted Child Society, 190 Rock Road, Glen Rock, NJ 07542 has served New Jersey gifted students for three decades. Executive Director Gina Ginsberg Riggs has generated reams of helpful guidelines for parents of gifted children and for advocacy groups. Her article in *Gifted Child Quarterly* (Summer 1984) is full of practical, useful advice. Here are some highlights:

1. Power. A parents' organization sent a questionnaire to all district superintendents, requesting information about gifted programs, knowing there weren't any. The society became known as an uninformed group of parents with a hostile questionnaire, and it took many years of "good behavior" to earn acceptance by educators. Moral: You cannot fight bureaucracy. Join it, then trigger change from within. Concentrate on making your education partners look good at every opportunity.
2. Purpose. Define your goals and purpose at the outset and work steadfastly toward them. A group without purpose will founder like a ship on the rocks.
3. Constitution. When people have differences of opinion, power struggles, and personality conflicts, a constitution reminds the group of its goals when individuals want to charge off in different directions. Perhaps have an attorney member help you frame a constitution; use the guidelines in the book *Robert's Rules of Order* as a working reference.
4. Leadership. Only a positive leader, combining personal strengths with the ability to facilitate the direction of the group, can guide an organization toward reaching goals. Choose leaders for leadership alone, not because they have friends in high places.

5. Evaluation. List your goals, evaluate your progress. Ask participants to rate every program on a questionnaire. Have committee chairs make evaluation part of every operating plan. Periodically assess the entire operation.

6. Strengths. List categories of work to be done on membership forms and ask members to check off areas in which they can help. Ask members to fill in their professions and hobbies so that when something needs to be done, the project manager will know to whom to turn. Members should be happy to help, knowing their children will benefit.

7. Rewards. Volunteers need good pay; they get it in recognition and praise.

8. Information. Effective advocacy can be boiled down to positive use of accurate information by a large number of people. Work closely with state coordinators, other groups in your state, and those in other states.

9. Money. Get members with financial experience to manage the group's funds. Publish a goal-oriented budget so people know why you need their dues. Exploit the knowledge and experience of your members to get the most for their money.

10. Growth. Change with the times. Organizations don't stand still; they grow and prosper or they slowly fade away.

11. Productive meetings. To be well attended, meetings should be enjoyable. Start on time, follow an agenda, and end early. Involve people personally; combine politeness and firmness to curb long-winded talkers. Give people time to enjoy themselves; it is their meeting, and you want them to come back.

In *An Advocate's Guide to Building Support for Gifted and Talented Education*, editor Patricia Bruce Mitchell cautions us about four "Pitfalls in Advocacy Efforts." The first is trying to be adversaries in the style of vocal minorities, which is no longer effective; the second is assuming that administrators are not too bright, which is destructive; being impatient is third; and, finally, being egotistical:

> The failure of many advocacy efforts . . . can be directly or indirectly traced to a common human malady: egoism. Perhaps the toughest challenge you will face as an advocate for the gifted and talented will not be to testify before a legislative committee, but to manage to get a group of fellow advocates to work together. Getting that chorus together will

require a lot of effort and selflessness so that no one voice rises above the others.

Teachers, principals, and administrators, like all people, prefer to do things for their friends. Friends are good listeners and understanding supporters; they pitch in and help, rather than stand back and criticize; and if there's an area where you truly need some progress, a caring friend can tell you about it and help you through the process.

Now your gifted group can do some of the creative thinking outlined in chapter 5. Define the process; define the problem (or need); identify solutions; choose a plan; implement it. You will need lots of information at each step, and your power base should be involved at every step. As long as the majority participates in the recommendations, you shouldn't be hampered by splinter groups, cliques, or factions who work at cross-purposes or chase rainbows.

If you have a plan that is affordable, workable, and flexible, you're likely to get a sympathetic hearing from principals and your school board. Set realistic goals. It's easier to sell candy to raise matching funds for a new computer than it is to float a bond issue to build a new library.

WORKING WITH YOUR BOARD OF EDUCATION

Ideally we should have an ongoing partnership with our school boards. A school system isn't like a savings bank, a place to deposit a 5-year-old so we can pick him up, with accrued interest, thirteen years later.

People who seek election to boards of education are usually people like you: with kids in the public school system, an interest in seeing good education for all in your district, and an eye for the best use of tax dollars. It's a mistake to think of them as a faceless, nameless group.

We're hard enough on school boards already. We tend to impose a double standard on them that we wouldn't want imposed on us. Consider:

- We want administrators with PhDs to run our districts with vision and imagination, but we squawk if the budgeted fuel allocation runs out after a long cold spell.

- We ask them to lure bright young teachers, while holding the line on salary increases; when our most imaginative and ambitious teachers accept more lucrative positions elsewhere, we say the administration lacks vision.
- We decry large classes, but are skeptical of bond issues to build additional classrooms. When enrollment is down we pressure the districts to consolidate schools and sell off empty buildings. Then when enrollment surges we criticize the board's lack of foresight.

Gina Ginsberg Riggs, of the Gifted Child Society, has compiled some suggestions for parents who want to take their case to the board of education:

- Be familiar with your board's policies describing philosophy, goals, and objectives. Remember that board members are probably concerned parents like you, investing their good efforts and time.
- Be a well-informed and supportive parent. Attend board meetings regularly and demonstrate your interest in quality education for *all* children.
- Find opportunities to meet your board members personally; know both your friends and enemies and discover who is "sitting on the fence" about gifted education. Then you'll know how many votes you'll have to convert to have a majority.
- When you want to bring a matter before your board, present it in writing, signed by a group of parents, with enough time for the members to do their homework without being put on the defensive.
- When you attend the board meeting it should be for information; don't ask questions to which you know the answers: A hostile board will not work with you.
- Offer to help on a study committee with board members to investigate your concerns and arrive at practical solutions.
- Dedicate yourself to this: you can do anything you want to do if you want it badly enough, if you are willing to work hard enough, and if you will have a little patience—but not too much!

One parents' group did quite nicely in establishing a foothold in a relatively short time. Their district of seven schools was running a pull-out program that really pulled out: they took gifted kids in vans from school to school, a process that took ninety minutes per session just in travel time. At the same time, budget cuts reduced some of the enhancements that made science interesting at some grade levels.

The parents' group, which until then had met mostly for programs dealing with how to parent gifted students, now took enrichment into its own hands and offered voluntary after-school programs for all students. Using dynamic teachers and qualified community people to offer interesting courses for six Fridays at a time, they jumped right in. Enrollment was open to all students whose parents were dues-paying members of the group. This meant that, as the programs became more popular, the membership swelled. Revenues from dues helped underwrite worthy but undersubscribed classes. Soon the parents' organization was a power base that had to be reckoned with. When the school threatened program cutbacks, the steering committee had paid-up membership lists of 350 families and a substantial slice of the constituency of the elected school board. The group opposed the cutback, and won; the board had to impose its cutbacks in other areas.

EVALUATING YOUR SCHOOL'S GIFTED PROGRAM

From time to time you'll want to evaluate whether your school's gifted program is meeting the needs of its students. Just as potential giftedness within a child is a process, so is its treatment within a school system. As times change, so can the needs of students. A program that worked wonders for its beneficiaries five years ago might not be speaking to the needs of their younger siblings.

With your fellow parents, run through this checklist:

Evaluation

- Are there stated goals defining what kind of giftedness will be addressed by the program?
- Is the incoming school population being carefully screened for likely prospects for the program? Are appropriate instruments being used?
- Are qualifying factors beyond simple IQ scores considered?

- Are parents informed of the program and the screening, and are they consulted for indications of giftedness they may have recognized in their children?
- Are screeners trained to look beyond the facets of giftedness identified by the screening instrument?
- Is there a clearly stated policy of entrance and exit criteria? Is inclusion possible throughout the year, not just in September? Can parents or students withdraw during the year if they choose?
- What percentage of the total population is included in the gifted program?
- Are students grouped by strengths in their specific areas?
- Are students from the program mainstreamed for part of each day?
- Is sufficient time allotted for the program (at least 150 minutes/week)?
- Does it make full use of community resources?
- Are teachers properly chosen and well trained?
- What is the ratio of students to teachers?
- Do students have the opportunity to contribute to the direction of the program?
- Do students have the opportunity for self-evaluation?
- Is the program well funded, and is it cost-efficient?
- Is higher-level thought encouraged?
- Is testing noncompetitive?
- Are creativity and divergent thought encouraged?
- Is creative problem-solving taught and practiced?
- Are presentations interdisciplinary?
- Can a student's progress in a subject continue without ceilings as long as he continues to grow?
- Is there continuity from year to year?
- Do students' evaluations get passed along at matriculation?
- Are students allowed to contribute ideas to guide planning?
- Is the program represented to other students and the community as an honor and a positive experience?

Other items may suggest themselves for your own checklist.

Once the program is in place, a broader administrative view is needed. Your school and school district should formulate and declare a policy for preparing staff for an ongoing program of education. Michael Horvich, Coordinator of the Talented and Gifted Program in the Glenview (IL) Public Schools, lists in the *Illinois Council for Gifted Journal*, Vol.

2, 1984, some of the questions administrators might ask as they chart their course:

- Is there money available to provide materials other than the basic ones used in the district?
- Is there money available to hire a coordinator or to send teachers to take courses after school or during the summer?
- Are teachers making enough money in their regular jobs to avoid the drain of moonlighting or financial worry?
- Are they free to devote full energy to both the classroom of 25–40 students and the learning disabled and gifted?
- Should there be required certification to teach the gifted?
- Should all teachers be required to take coursework on the gifted during their college career?
- Do we reach the gifted within the regular classroom, do we pull them out, do we group them heterogeneously?
- What about the curriculum? What should we teach them? Or should we be more interested in thinking and process than fact learning or product?

Parents of students in the program should encourage school administrators to consider every part of this facet of program planning.

Your child's education is a partnership from the first day of school until the last commencement exercise twelve, sixteen, or more years later. You and your school are partners, not adversaries. Neither of you can do the job as well entirely without the other; the situation calls for compromise, not combat. Your child begins as a junior partner, and the outcome eventually depends on his investment as well as yours and your school's. Perhaps no other partnership so richly deserves our finest efforts at cooperation and shared enterprise.

9

Supplementing Your Child's Formal Education

Enriching your child's environment is in some ways like planning your family's meals for the coming week. We get most of our food from one or two supermarkets, asking them to stock things we need or like if we don't find them on the shelves. Then we stop at roadside stands for fresh produce when it's available; we go across town for something that looks especially good but isn't in our neighborhood. We get occasional prime cuts at a butcher shop, and if conditions are right we grow some of our own produce. When we plan meals from day to day, we plan for variety and balance, keeping in mind individual preferences and diet restrictions.

As we bring up our children, we rely as well on our local schools for as much as they can offer from day to day. When they don't have a program we would like, we ask them to add it. But we go across town for supplementation; we splurge for a special treat once in a while, and we sow many of our own seeds at home. We look to church, theater, print and electronic media, and movies for nurturance. We introduce variety and allow for individual preferences and needs. Sometimes we feel starved or stuffed; often we crave a little spice.

Before we look at some of the things families can do on their own initiative, let's consider formal weekend programs already in place and their impact on the gifted families who patronize them. Because many institutions and parents' groups have inquired about them, and interest is always strong at professional conventions, quite possibly a program modeled along these lines would be effective and well subscribed to in your community.

Naturally, what kind of supplement you look for will depend on what your child already gets in his school system. This may also vary from year to year, depending on his interests and stage of development. Your school may have an award-winning science and math department but precious little to offer a creative writer. Another school might have world-class performing arts talent, but your child may tell you he's picked the math department clean by November of sophomore year. Or perhaps your daughter may have stacks of books to challenge her math concepts but be the only person in your school with an IQ of 150—so she says she'd like to feel normal once in a while and talk to somebody her age who's at her level. Perhaps your son wishes he could mention "hero" to a boy his age without getting a Hulk toy shoved in his face.

If any of these sound like your home, reach for the car keys. It's time to find an enrichment program or enlist other parents of gifted children and launch one of your own.

Many gifted programs tend to lean toward either the creative end or the academic end of the spectrum. Both have their place. The academic programs focus on specific enrichment in traditional disciplines: math, sciences, foreign languages, history. The creative ones may offer cooking, futuristics—the modeling of long-range solutions to meet social needs—storytelling, and drama as a way to teach thinking skills and creativity.

Gifted children are especially interested in active inquiry and problem solving in social studies and sciences and in creative expression in the arts. A curriculum too narrowly focused on mastery of basic skills in reading, writing, and math, with much repetitive drill, can turn off gifted children. That's when a supplementary program can fill in the gaps and round out your child's development.

In recent years, entry age in programs like these has dropped to primary and even preschool levels. Let's take a closer look.

To learn about language that predates written alphabets, 4- and 5-year-olds were doing cave paintings like cavemen. What excited these children was that they could see the evolution of language. One said, when he saw a photo of cave art in Europe, "That's just like me when I was 3!" He made his own link between the world's evolution of language and his own. Such experiences make learning fun for bright children—and, we must say, for their teachers.

In our gifted enrichment programs, sponsored by the National College of Education, in Evanston, Illinois, we meet several kindergarten dropouts—kids who have a sense of not being really happy with kindergarten—but since they haven't experienced anything else, they think that's what all school is like until they try one of our programs. They seem to say, "OK, I've got socialization down pat, now what can we find for me to *think about?*"

Children who are especially bright enjoy being with other gifted children, and make a lot of friends among their intellectual peers. Small-group work and team projects provide directed socialization. For example, in the National College of Education's weekend and summer programs, preschoolers are paired up to present stories to the larger group; to build something such as a "fantastic machine;" or work on an art or math project together.

In these programs the 4-year-olds move from room to room between their chosen classes, just like high school students. They use color-coded schedule cards on their name tags so they can find their classrooms and match up with classmates, and so program personnel can supervise their comings and goings. The key to the success of such programs, which handle more than 100 4- and 5-year-olds at a time, is plenty of good adult supervision, along with help from older children and a "buddy system." Classes are no larger than twelve to a teacher, allowing for lots of individual projects and small-group work not found in typical kindergartens.

The curriculum is advanced, offering subjects such as the sciences and math, which are often absent from or oversimplified in regular preschool and kindergarten curricula. These courses are among the most frequently requested by the children. For example, for 4s and 5s there are: Kitchen Chemists; One Inch Small—One Mile High, and for first through sixth graders there are Geometric Design: String, Thread, and Yarn; Integrative Math: Logic, Patterns, and Constructions; Microbiology; Geology: Journey to the Center of the Earth; Chemistry: Air, Water and Fire; and Light: A Spectrum of Creative and Scientific Activities.

Courses emphasize thinking skills; for example, one class learned about parts of a newspaper as they pretended to report, write, and produce a paper of their own. Another replicated an all-night diner in the classroom and children role-played people who work all night, such as nurses, policemen, janitors, construction workers, bakers, and reporters. The children talked about the early morning hours and how the world doesn't really stand still while most people sleep. Together they wrote a book and a poem, and made pancakes for the "night workers."

Creative science activities the preschoolers enjoyed on weekends included:

- Building a 14-foot-tall giraffe in a cooperative effort.
- Categorizing insects and role-playing the parts of several of them.
- Examining fossil bones and trying to imagine what the rest of the creature was like; talking about excavations and digging; making up their own labels for dinosaurs.
- Contrasting and comparing audio "soundscapes" from a country meadow and from the city.

Activities like these express originality and imagination, and each becomes a catalyst for new views and depths of understanding, not just making a drawing or model of a dinosaur or giraffe, but forming new ways of seeing the world. The children grow accustomed to inventing new objects and activities.

Ideally, several of the concepts below will be components of the preschool or primary enrichment program you choose:

- Exposure to a wide variety of individualized, hands-on activities, particularly in the sciences and math, and problem solving based on logical reasoning and hypothetical thinking.
- Creating writing classes that emphasize personal expression and more vivid and sophisticated word usage and creative description than do basic prereading and prewriting activities in regular schools.
- Fun topics that stimulate the imagination, such as a class on the pyramids of ancient Egypt. It may be several years before they get into serious study of such topics, but this early experience gives children something to chew on while they practice their thinking skills.

Consider programs that leave your child with time to play and interact with peers rather than struggle to stay abreast of factual material. Programs that offer a wide variety of options help support his development as a whole person. Your math star may love a musical theater class as a change of pace; your avid reader-writer might enjoy cooking up a chemical casserole.

Balance is the key once again. Too many organized activities can be as harmful as too much unstructured time. Still, good enrichment programs can be important because most 4- and 5-year-olds aren't able to provide stimulating, organized activities for themselves on a consistent basis. Keep the atmosphere enriched but give the children room to breathe.

Before you put your child in a program, get a sense of the philosophy of the people who direct it—the balance they strive for between the academic and the creative; whether they really care for and have an affection for the children; are the children able to have activities away from their seats? Do the teachers rely on lots of paper work? Are the children expected to read and write?

Overly specific academic goals may indicate overintensity; beware of promises to "move your child ahead one grade level" or to "prepare him for this test."

The last word on your child's participation may be body language. Does she return drained or is she smiling and bursting with things to talk about? Is she having fun or is it tough? Does the session seem too long or too short?

Some summer programs accommodate children all day, with academic activities in the morning and optional outdoor physical activities in the afternoon. Outdoor education can include nature programs, field trips to museums or concerts, cooperative games, outdoor art, cooking, and gardening.

Many gifted programs are run by colleges and universities as part of their education departments. Others are functions of school districts, government agencies, private organizations and foundations, park districts, and private parents' groups.

The parents' group we mentioned in the last chapter organized a trial afterschool program to see if there was interest in the community. It was instantly successful and ran for several years. The class organizer recalls,

We offered some fun courses in art, science, creative writing, storytelling, whatever teachers or parents thought would be useful. The superintendent let us use schoolrooms at no cost. Then we put out flyers and offered a choice of six afterschool classes for $10 per subject.

The program was a hit. At its peak we had twenty-five classes filled, three sessions a school year, and the day we sent out registration materials people would come running to our house to be sure of getting their first choice. Everything filled up in five days. Any child could come, but the family had to be members of our group, at $10 a year. We didn't require testing, just parent nomination and sincere motivation by the kids; we weren't a baby-sitting service.

It was sheer fun, all the way. The kids had a ball. We had stained-glass artists, a sculptor, a puppeteer. Teachers offered to work with us. The science classes did rocketry, and math courses plotted the rocket trajectory.

I couldn't believe all the support we got. Parents couldn't have been nicer. If we needed anything they volunteered. Everybody was so grateful. We came away just high after classes. In all the years we didn't have one complaint.

Remember that a program doesn't have to be labeled "gifted" to be good. Hundreds of other opportunities may be found in your community and the surrounding area. Lessons in an artistic area—dance, music, art—may encourage persistence and self-evaluation. Some community team sports are more appropriate than others; activities like swimming and soccer are sometimes less rigidly subject to star systems and therefore more inclusive of beginners. (Some win-or-die experiences are just what the gifted perfectionist doesn't need.)

Courses by park districts, museums, libraries, and YMCAs can offer enrichment. Scouting and Campfire programs can develop leadership skills, social skills, teamwork, self-reliance, and initiative. Working toward merit badges can expose your child to new interests and allow him to gain recognition for achievement in a non-competitive atmosphere.

But remember, you're working for balance. Don't overschedule your child. Watch to see what best fits his needs at the moment. No child should be involved in *all* the things we've mentioned.

VERITY BEGINS AT HOME

Don't feel that your guide to supplementing formal education has to be the Yellow Pages. We've maintained all through this book that children's principal source of enrichment is an imaginative, diversified home and family.

Investigate what's available at teachers' supply stores and children's bookstores for materials that encourage the development of thinking processes, not just academic knowledge. Activities should be open-ended ones, not merely one-dimensional workbook exercises that don't teach thinking skills. Some workbooks teach children little more than how to fill in workbooks.

Parents need to encourage children's learning at home, offer helpful, positive feedback, and keep books and materials around the house. Unusual enthusiasm on the part of parents for a particular talent is important in the development of exceptional talents among children. But that enthusiasm must be sincere to have a productive result and must conform to children's interests and needs. Forcing children to practice the piano for too long when they're too young may only result in their giving it up as soon as they can.

Look too for tutors and teachers on the basis of their enthusiasm and energy and their ability to keep ahead of the bright child. Willingness and capacity to work hard are probably the biggest factors in identifying an outstanding tutor or role model for a gifted child's developing talents.

Social anthropologist Margaret Mead in *Blackberry Winter* remembers her own childhood mentors:

> Mother thought about every place we lived not only in terms of its schools, but also as a more or less promising source of "lessons." Whatever form such lessons took—drawing, painting, carving, modeling or basketry—she thought of them as a supplement to formal education within the context of the most advanced educational theories. In Hammonton I had music lessons and also lessons in carving, because the only artist the town boasted was a skilled woodcarver. In Swarthmore we were taught by an all-round manual training teacher under whose tutelage I even built a small loom. In Bucks County I had painting lessons from a local artist and later from an artist in New Hope. And one year Mother had a local carpenter teach Dick and me woodworking. She was completely eclectic about what we were taught in these lessons, provided the person who was teaching us was highly skilled.

When the motivation comes from within the child, she can make use of the "work" of play to establish her own sense of competency.

10

The End of the Beginning

In the preceding nine chapters we've tried to lay the foundation for an understanding of the process we call giftedness. We don't pretend to have all the answers, but rather we hope we have encouraged you to look for them as questions arise in your child's early years.

GIFTEDNESS AND BIRTH ORDER

One of the subjects we've dealt with is how to discover potential giftedness among very young children. Believe it or not, for many years many people thought giftedness was something that happened to firstborn or only children. Most major studies showed that more than half of the children identified as gifted were in either of these categories. But Linda Silverman describes her findings at the Gifted Child Development Center in Denver:

> In 1981, all of this research thoroughly convinced us that giftedness visited first-borns to a greater extent than anyone else in the family. Then something interesting happened to challenge this belief. Some parents brought in their "nongifted" second children to be tested, quite convinced that the younger siblings were not gifted. They wanted to gain information about the children's learning styles which they found valuable in the

assessment of their eldest. To everyone's astonishment, the second children came out within a few IQ points of their older siblings.

The parents were surprised because these second-born children didn't act gifted; that is, they didn't behave or achieve like the firstborns, who walked right out of the textbooks.

In Silverman's subsequent study of 148 families in which the eldest was identified as gifted, all but twelve percent of the younger siblings tested no more than thirteen IQ points below their eldest sibling. Some of the wider IQ ranges in the remaining twelve percent were traced to auditory processing problems linked to chronic ear infections, and to the difference in age at the time tests were administered to each sibling. In more than a third of the test families, the siblings' IQ scores ranged within five points, close to the margin of error in some tests. For all practical purposes the IQ was the same; the behavior was different.

Parents described firstborn and only children as "perfectionistic, achieving, adult-like, leaders, reliable, well-organized, critical, conforming to adult expectations, serious." These are traits often used to label high-achievers, who are more likely to be identified as gifted than their similarly gifted but more laid-back siblings.

In her monograph, "The Second Child Syndrome," Silverman theorizes that older children convey a simple, unambiguous message to their younger siblings: "Remember, I'm the boss around here, so don't mess with my turf or you're in big trouble." The younger children quickly learn the rules of the game and try to be as nonthreatening as possible while consciously choosing and developing different, noncompetitive areas of interest. As pack animals accede to the dominant member, younger children often yield to unwritten claims staked out on areas of interest by their elder siblings; if number one is big in music and math, number two will dabble in everything but those "protected" fields.

Silverman finds that the self-concept of younger siblings often suffers in comparison with that of their elders. They, if not others, consider themselves to be the "nongifted" ones in their families. Recognizing and developing their distinct talents and giftedness brings harmony to the family and helps develop healthy self-concepts in all the children.

Parents of the high-achievers in Benjamin Bloom's study reported in *Developing Talent in Young People* conceded that younger siblings' careers and personal development sometimes took a back seat to those of the elder because of the hardship of traveling to practice and performance, the cost of training, and the general commotion surrounding the subject children.

GIFTEDNESS AND GENDER

A very sensitive dynamic exists among gifted children. Sometimes it almost seems that there is a magic revolving door through which they pass. When they emerge from the other side they seem to be quite different people: you might even say some of them no longer appear to be exceptional at all.

Barbara Clark's third edition of *Growing Up Gifted* (1988) summarizes:

> While IQ bears a fairly close relationship to accomplishment among men, it bears essentially no relationship among women, with two-thirds of the women with IQs of 170 or above occupied as housewives or office workers. . . . In technical and professional fields the representation of gifted and talented women has actually experienced a decline since the early 1900s.

Clark sites a study reported in *Time* magazine (July 12, 1982):

- More than one-third of all MBA candidates are women, but only five percent of the executives in the top fifty American companies are women;
- In the profession traditionally dominated by women, education—
  Eighty percent of all elementary principals are men
  Ninety-six percent of all junior high principals are men
  Ninety-nine and nine tenths percent of all school superintendents are men
  Seventy percent of all classroom teachers are women, but they earn an average of $3000 per year *less* than their male counterparts.

A 1987 article by Sally Reis: "We can't change what we don't recognize: Understanding the special needs of gifted females," in *Gifted Child Quarterly*, Spring 1987, establishes that "data reported in 1987 show virtually no gains in these statistics."

A major barrier to higher-paying careers for women has been the lack of more comprehensive mathematics preparation in their careers. Barbara Clark quotes a 1984 study by C. K. Rekdal, "Guiding the gifted female through being aware: The math connection," showing that

> less than 12% of women entering the University of California system today have the high school math prerequisites that would allow them to participate in 80% of the majors offered by that system. According to Rekdal gifted females do not pursue math even when they express levels of interest in math and perform as well as males.

Why?
"From the beginning," continues Clark,

> girls are taught to be passive, accepting, nurturing. They are expected to enjoy quieter games and activities and not to take risks. They receive these messages from many places and many people in our society. . . . We know that gifted children tend to develop more quickly than more typical children, and we find that gifted girls usually develop even more quickly in the first few years. . . . This may cause devastating loneliness for sensitive girls of high potential. When, as youths, these girls try to show their ability, they are accused of being bossy, unfeminine, and show-offs, so they tend to withdraw.

A very thoughtful and helpful book by Barbara Kerr, *Smart Girls, Gifted Women,* deals with the problems and solutions that gifted girls encounter. The aspect that sparked the research was her observation that gifted girls with strong performance in the lower grades drop off later and seem to develop lower career expectations.

Kerr has specific suggestions for parents of gifted girls in preschool through postgraduate years. The scope of our book is the early years, so we'll summarize some of what she says about that period.

Preschool

Save the frilly dresses, pastels, and lace for special occasions. Dress your daughter for school and play in bright colors if she likes and durable, comfortable, active clothes.

Choose nonsexist toys, not trucks for boys versus dolls for girls. Encourage quiet nurturing play, sure, but don't discourage more active play.

Choose your child care cautiously, avoiding centers that segregate by gender. Don't let them enforce actual sleep rigidly; gifted girls seem to need quiet time alone but not sleep. Make sure there are lots of books with lots of time for looking at them. Observe sessions and watch for sex-role treatment.

Take care to show your gifted girl your workplace and explain what you do and how it fits into the scheme of things.

Have her tested privately, whether for early admission to school or inclusion in a gifted program, or for an assessment of her strengths and a benchmark of her abilities compared to other children.

Take advantage of preschool programs that may provide intellectual stimulation, but don't push.

Choose television programs, and watch out for gender stereotypes. Take time to explain what you're seeing and bring it into the context of your home.

Answer any and all questions; have special uninterrupted time with your child each day.

Primary School

Many gifted girls read by kindergarten; have books everywhere and provide the free time to enjoy them. Have lots of books that portray women in many roles. Help her read when she asks.

Do puzzles for math-oriented minds. You may need a computer at home. Camping, hiking, short trips all broaden her horizons. Novelty and adventure are required.

Schedule free time, for daydreaming, looking out the window, imagining. Don't push friendships, which will or won't come of their own volition.

Watch for stress signs about school. They suggest she needs more stimulation or opportunity; she might not complain or act out as a boy might.

Role models are important, even in baby-sitters.

Intense emotions need support even when they're hard for parents to take. Let her know you're behind her all the way.

Help her feel important, unique, special. Always be honest. Don't hide her abilities from her.

PARENTING: A CREATIVE ART

Having dealt with certain stages of child development and certain aspects of children's behavior and abilities, let's tie the parts together and treat them as an ongoing process, which, of course, is what they are.

As parents, one of our first tasks is to set the stage for the creation of a healthy self-image and a strong self-concept. Our children learn to have faith in their ability to guide their own growth, and they initiate course changes along the way.

We provide appropriate stimulation, an atmosphere that encourages growth, and opportunity to flourish in a protective surrounding. Then we maintain a constant overview, not turning everything over to our school system, but helping keep things on course as professional educators take over the helm.

Interestingly enough, the maintenance of self-confidence is something our parents, schools, and cultures have taught us to do in the worst possible way.

PRAISE VERSUS ENCOURAGEMENT

Just as we coo at a baby, we are acculturated to squeal "good boy" or "good girl" and applaud when baby takes a step or connects a spoonful of strained carrots with her mouth. Now the evidence suggests that this is all wrong, no matter how right it feels to us when we're doing it.

Randy Hitz, PhD, an early childhood specialist for the Oregon Department of Education, and Amy Driscoll, Ed.D, associate professor of early childhood education/teacher education at Portland State University, summarize findings from several researchers in their article, "Praise or Encouragement? New Insights into Praise: Implications for Early Childhood Teachers," in the July, 1988, issue of *Young Children*. [Authors' Note: Citations in this article include: Brophy, J.E., 1981; Stokes, T., Fowler, S., & Baer, D., 1978; Esler, W.K., 1983; Martin, D.L., 1977; Stringer, B.R. & Hurt, H.T., 1981; Green, D., & Lepper, M.R., 1974; Ohanian, S., 1982.] Here is what professionals find about this style of praise:

- It sets up failure by implying that acceptance is conditional upon proper completion of a task.

- It lowers children's confidence, training them to watch for constant signs of approval or disapproval.
- It teaches children not to take chances or attempt difficult tasks, so as to avoid having praise withheld.
- It singles out the successful at the expense of the unsuccessful.
- It teaches some children to be adept at pulling praise from teachers or parents.
- It teaches children to be dependent on external approval.
- It becomes a manipulative tool for the adult, who may dole it out pointedly as an object lesson to another child who is not behaving.

What should a parent or teacher do, then?

Encourage. Don't praise, encourage. Offer positive reinforcement along the way to help channel efforts, but not as a reward for pleasing you at the end of the line.

This is praise: "You did a good job. You are a good boy. What a good reader you are! You are Mommy's best little helper. I love your picture. That's a great report card. You are so smart! I'm happy when you're good for the sitter."

This is encouragement: "You are reading more words now. You put lots of birds in that picture. Your block tower is really tall. You used a lot of toothpicks in your sculpture. You worked a long time on that castle. You made real progress in both math *and* science this semester. Sitter said you picked up your toys and went to bed right on time last night."

Praise bestows external value for external qualities. Encouragement acknowledges effort while leaving appraisal to the artist. Praise singles out in public; encouragement acknowledges in private. Encouragement focuses on process and improvement, where praise gets heaped upon the product. Praise is often general; encouragement is specific.

All this may seem hard to differentiate, but it is not a new idea. Praise misused as a motivator was identified and discouraged by Piaget in the 1950s, by Maria Montessori in the 1960s, by Haim Ginott in the 1970s, and by Theodor Dreikurs in the 1980s.

We admit that replacing praise with encouragement is no simple substitution. Yet powerful evidence shows that removing praise opens doors to risk taking and self-evaluation and persistence, each of which is a key productive behavior among gifted children. We owe it to our children to make such modifications in our own behavior as are necessary to enable their fullest development.

If a case study can help demonstrate the need, let it be this one: popular pediatrician T. Berry Brazelton in *On Becoming a Family* wrote of a study of mother-infant modeling in Western Kenya. Contrast this style with the typical praise feast we described above.

Researchers set up a situation in which Kenyan mothers were to "teach" their babies a task from the Bayley standardized infant activity exam. The mother would model the entire task, then sit back and wait for the infant to try it, saying repeatedly and monotonously to him, "you can do it . . . you can do it . . . you can do it." When he performed the first stage of the task the mother would become completely silent, giving the baby the opportunity and time to realize *he* had done it; the baby became excited, the mother urged him on. At the next stage of success the mother would be silent again.

Does this teaching style sound foreign to you? Consider that in Kenya average babies demonstrate advanced reaching behavior, sit alone at 4 months, and walk well at 9 months.

Brazelton concludes:

> We began to view positive reinforcement very differently after this. Depending on *how* it's used, it can be very manipulative and it can become a way of stripping an infant of his own choices and sense of achievement. At least in this comparison, it was obvious that U.S. mothers were more controlling with their reinforcement, and the opportunity for the baby to realize his own autonomous achievement was diluted.
>
> By the time a mother has taught her baby how to control inner states and how to direct and prolong his attention it is time to turn the control back to him, both subtly and overtly.
>
> The purest sign of attachment is the ability to detach at appropriate stages in the infant's development. This is critical to his ability to act for himself and to learn about the excitement of autonomy. Autonomous achievements are the foundation for the baby's own belief in himself—and form the ingredients of his ego. . . . There seem to be critical stages for fostering independence.

SELF-CONCEPT: A DELICATE BALANCE

As your child moves through grade school, her self-concept is shaped more and more in relation to the other children in her classroom. If your school "mainstreams" its intellectually gifted throughout the general population, she may enjoy being the first to master new material, being the one for whom perfect scores are not out of reach, and being able to coast with minimal effort. Eventually, though, a setting like this becomes stifling, as challenges are few and the material isn't stimulating. The lone intellectually gifted child may feel lost and outcast in a classroom where nobody can keep up with her. One or two gifted children in a class of twenty-four might grow to feel superior to their less-advanced neighbors, an attitude that should not be encouraged. Sometimes the other children misinterpret the nature of giftedness and perceive those children as somehow not "normal."

This picture can change when gifted children are grouped together. The child who thought she was "different" now finds herself among peers, where it's normal to be exceptional. Now she can relax and be herself without the disguise she may have devised in order to "fit in" among her classmates. She may find the atmosphere challenging and stimulating, or she may feel threateneed to be surrounded by equals and suddenly dependent on her wits to hold her own. This can be a growth experience too!

In this setting the child might abandon risk-taking behavior in order to feel safe. In any case the balance may be delicate, and parents and professionals alike should be alert for any behavioral change.

"Children who demonstrate very positive self-concepts, strong egos and a tendency toward impatience with others of lesser ability may be more appropriately placed in a homogeneous group of [gifted] students, which is apt to be more humbling as well as more challenging," writes Margie Kitano, associate dean for faculty development and research, College of San Diego, San Diego State University, in *Intellectual Giftedness and Young Children: Recognition and Development*.

UNDERACHIEVEMENT

For a number of reasons, some of which are perfectly understandable if indefensible, some academically gifted students burn out or tune out instead of performing at their externally perceived "level of ability." Parents and teachers then may be tempted to lecture about "living up to your potential," which by extension can become motivation by guilt, which may work when housebreaking a cocker spaniel but rarely succeeds among gifted children. Parents grow exasperated, teachers may feel threatened instead of challenged, and children may subsequently spiral downward. This syndrome is altogether too common among middle- and higher-grade children, but it can be seen in younger ones as well.

Preventive steps can minimize the effect and reset the child's course before the situation gets out of hand. In *Underachievement Syndrome: Causes and Cures*, Sylvia Rimm makes specific suggestions to help parents prevent underachievement before it begins. The most important preventive measure, Rimm feels, is providing the child with appropriate role models.

> Not only should you be achieving persons, but you must share with your children a realistic and positive view of achievement. They must see the components of achievement and especially the ways in which efforts and outcomes are related. They must understand that you sometimes fail, but that you survive that failure to succeed again. . . . They must view the intrinsic and extrinsic rewards that come with effort.

Rimm cautions parents to avoid complaints about their spouse's work. Common pitfalls to avoid are a mother's complaints about her husband's long hours or difficult bosses and the father's devaluation of his wife's career or of her contributions as a homemaker or community volunteer.

A second area of import mentioned by Rimm is the need for parents to maintain control and teach children to accept some limitations.

> Empowering children with adult-decision-making provides power without wisdom. It leads to formidable and continuing conflicts between children and their parents as they compete for the power that parents give too early and try to recover too late.

Parents, notes Rimm, need to impart clear positive messages to their children about expectations for achievement both in school and out. Consistency is important both over time and between parents. Children need to learn how to function in competition, especially how to recover after losses. And they should also be involved in some noncompetitive activities which are intrinsically rewarding. Finally, Rimm recommends that parents "model and teach reasonable organizational techniques as they relate to home and school responsibilities."

Rimm's book lists specific remedies for both parents and teachers to help reverse underachievement patterns that have already become established. However, in the case of older children and those underachievement patterns Rimm describes as "dominant and nonconforming," she cautions that the assistance of psychologists or counselors may be necessary.

Dr. Linda Silverman of the Gifted Child Development Center in Denver, in a paper entitled "Reaching Underachievers," points out another case of underachievement in gifted children during the early school years. Achieving gifted children, Silverman states,

> tend to be good sequential learners while gifted underachievers frequently have high spatial abilities and underdeveloped sequencing skills. While their spatial skills help them in such areas as computers, geometry, science and visual memory, these underachievers have difficulty remembering three-step directions and learning such subjects as phonics, spelling, foreign languages and math facts in the way in which these subjects are usually taught. Early diagnosis and a change in teaching methods can help these children from establishing an underachievement pattern.

Rather than blaming the child or the teacher, Joanne Rand Whitmore, in "Understand a Lack of Motivation to Excel," an article in *Gifted Child Quarterly*, Spring 1986, suggests we place equal or greater responsibility on the external environments of school and home. She offers these premises:

1. Young gifted children have superior ability to adapt behavior and solve problems.
2. Personal characteristics that become problems are the inappropriate manifestations of qualities we normally call strengths (such as perfectionism).
3. Problem behaviors are efforts to cope with an environment that doesn't meet children's needs.
4. Underachievement is reversible when adults provide an *early* and appropriate educational environment.

The parent's role, in this situation and always, is to foster self-confidence. The child who thinks poorly of himself will generally not pull himself out of a tailspin. Properly encouraged, the child who believes he can modify his behavior to his own standards, probably can. When others exhort him to measure up to their standards, however, he may not make the effort.

CONTINUITY

In this book we've talked about stages of development that we can define and limit in time. We've also dealt with characteristics of behavior like creativity and intelligence. But, really, it's ambitious and artificial to try to isolate either the moment or the essence of behavior, because they're interwoven from the start, quite interdependent and indistinguishable within the process.

When our children are born we watch for the transition from each stage of development to the next. We modify our behavior as we perceive their needs and as their individuality becomes manifest. With each step, we build upon our experience and the insights we've gained. So it is through infancy, when we are everything our children need; the toddler stage, when they begin to discover their ability to explore; the preschool years, when the self continues to emerge; and the transition to formal schooling.

This process does not cease on the first day of school . . . nor, for that matter, the last. With every step in every school—preschool to kindergarten, to primary, to intermediary, between districts, or out-of-state—the parent must maintain an overview of educational programs. The fourth-grade program should build on and extend the abilities encouraged by the program or teacher in the primary grades. Continuity is essential to smooth development.

Review your child's needs at each level within the school and at each step in her maturing—as interests and styles change. Is the school on target or missing by a mile? If it's missing, it's time to consider again an active pursuit of enrichment. What subjects look good to your child? Might she meet some new, like-minded friends to encourage more growth? Is there a new topic or area that she'd like to pursue? Be ready to intervene any time the school and its program are not meeting her needs. If an impossible situation cannot be circumvented, perhaps only home schooling will be adequate. Be ready to mobilize as your child's advocate. The groundwork you're laying will last a lifetime.

Bruno Bettelheim wrote in *The Good Enough Parent*:

> A parent must continually and flexibly adapt his procedures to the responses of his child, and reassess the everchanging overall situation as it develops . . .
> Raising children is a creative endeavor, an art rather than a science.

The dividend from the time and effort you're investing will be sizable, and there are many rewards along the way: the fresh insights your children bring, the joys of creation they share, the exaltation of accomplishment that is theirs and yours.

Further Reading

General Parenting

Beck, Joan. *How to Raise a Brighter Child.* New York: Trident, 1967.

Bettelheim, Bruno. *A Good Enough Parent: A Book on Child-Rearing.* New York: Alfred A. Knopf, 1987.

Brazelton, T. Berry, M.D. *Infants and Mothers: Differences in Development.* rev. ed. New York: Delacorte Press/Seymour Lawrence Inc., 1983.

Butler, Dorothy. *Babies Need Books.* New York: Atheneum, 1980, 1982; Penguin Books, 1982.

Dreikurs, Rudolf. *Children: The Challenge.* New York: E. P. Dutton, 1964.

Dyer, Wayne W., Dr. *What Do You Really Want for Your Children?* New York: William Morrow & Co., 1985.

Engelhardt, Anne, and Sullivan, Anne. *Playful Learning: An Alternate Approach to Preschool.* Franklin Park, IL: La Leche League Intl., 1986.

Fraiberg, S. H. *The Magic Years.* New York: Scribner's Sons, 1959.

Healy, Jane M. *Your Child's Growing Mind: A Parent's Guide to Learning from Birth to Adolescence.* Garden City, NY: Doubleday, 1987.

Keirsey, David. *Portraits of Temperament.* Del Mar, CA: Prometheus Nemesis Book Co., 1988.

Keirsey, David, and Bates, Marilyn. *Please Understand Me: Character and Temperament Types.* Del Mar, CA: Prometheus Nemesis Book Co., 1984.

White, Burton L. *Educating the Infant and Toddler.* Lexington, MA: Lexington Books/D. C. Heath & Co., 1988.

———. *The First Three Years of Life.* rev. ed. New York: Prentice-Hall, 1985.

Activities and Ideas for Parents

Braun, Sam Ed. *Bubbles, Rainbows and Worms: Science Experiments for Pre-school Children.* Mt. Rainier, MD: Gryphon House, Inc., 1981.

Cook, Carole, and Carlisle, Jody. *Challenges for Children: Creative Activities for Gifted and Talented Primary Students*. West Nyack, NY: Center for Applied Research in Education, Inc., 1985.

Faggella, Kathy. *Concept Cookery: Learning Concepts Through Cooking*. Bridgeport, CT: First Teacher Press, (1985).

Institute for Child Behavior and Development, University of Illinois. *Nurturing Talent in the Visual and Performing Arts in Early Childhood: Art and Music*. Urbana, IL: University of Illinois Press, 1978.

Kane, Jane A. *Art Through Nature: An Integrated Approach to Teaching Art and Nature Study to Young Children*. Holmes Beach, FL: Learning Publications, Inc., 1985.

Redleaf, Rhoda. *Open the Door, Let's Explore: Neighborhood Trips for Your Children*. St. Paul, MN: Toys 'n' Things Press, 1984.

Silberstein-Storfer, Muriel, with Jones, Mablen. *Doing Art Together*. New York: Simon & Schuster, 1982.

Smithsonian Learning Project. *Science Activity Book*. New York: Galison Books, 1987.

Striker, Susan. *Please Touch: How to Stimulate Your Child's Creative Development Through Movement, Music, Art and Play*. New York: Simon & Schuster, 1986.

Williams, Emily Needham. *High Tech Babies . . . An Owner's Manual: How to Encourage Your Child's Early Interest in Science and Math*. Dallas, TX: Presswords, 1986.

Zaslavsky, Claudia. *Preparing Young Children for Math: A Book of Games*. New York: Schocken Books, 1979.

Basic Books About the Gifted

Alvino, James, and eds. of Gifted Children Monthly. *Parents' Guide to Raising a Gifted Child*. Boston: Little, Brown & Co., 1985.

Galbraith, Judy. *The Gifted Kid's Survival Guide*. (*For Ages Ten and Under* [Companion book is available for ages 11-18]). Minneapolis, MN: Free Spirit Publishing, 1984.

Ginsberg, Gina, and Harrison, Charles. *How to Help Your Gifted Child: A Handbook for Parents and Teachers*. New York: Monarch Press, 1977.

Hall, Eleanor G., and Skinner, Nancy. *Somewhere to Turn: Strategies for Parents of the Gifted and Talented*. New York: Teachers College Press, 1980.

Kerr, Barbara. *Smart Girls, Gifted Women*. Columbus, OH: Ohio Psychological Publishing, 1985.

Miller, Bernard S., and Price, Merle, eds. *The Gifted, the Family, and the Community.* New York: Walker and Company, 1981.

Moore, L. P. *Does This Mean My Kid's a Genius?* New York: McGraw Hill Book Co., 1981.

Perino, Sheila C., and Perino, Joseph. *Parenting the Gifted: Developing the Promise.* New York: R. R. Bowker Co., 1981.

Saunders, Jacqulyn, with Espeland, Pamela. *Bringing Out the Best.* Minneapolis, MN: Free Spirit Publishing, 1986.

Vail, Priscilla. *The World of the Gifted Child.* New York: Walker and Co., 1979.

Webb, James T., Meckstroth, E., and Tolan, S. *Guiding the Gifted Child: A Practical Source for Parents and Teachers.* Columbus, OH: Ohio Psychological Publishing Co., 1982.

Serious Reading for Parents and Educators

Bloom, Benjamin, ed., et al. *Developing Talent in Young People.* New York: Ballantine Books, 1985.

Clark, Barbara. *Growing Up Gifted.* rev. ed. Columbus, OH: Merrill Publishing Co., 1988.

———. *Optimizing Learning: The Integrative Model in the Classroom* Columbus, OH: Merrill Publishing Co., 1986.

Edwards, Carolyn Pope, with Ramsey, Patricia G. *Promoting Social and Moral Development in Young Children: Creative Approaches for the Classroom.* New York: Teachers College Press, 1986.

Gallagher, James J. *Teaching the Gifted Child.* Boston: Allyn and Bacon, Inc., 1975.

Gardner, Howard. *Frames of Mind.* New York: Basic Books, 1983.

Goertzel, Victor, and Goertzel, Mildred G. *Cradles of Eminence.* Boston: Little, Brown & Co., 1962.

——— and Goertzel, Ted. *Three Hundred Eminent Personalities.* San Francisco, CA: Jossey-Bass, Inc., 1978.

Granger, Lori, and Granger, Bill. *The Magic Feather.* New York: E. P. Dutton, 1986.

Guilford, J. P. *Creative Talents: Their Nature, Uses and Development.* Buffalo, NY: Bearly Limited, 1986.

Hajcak, F., and Garwood, P. *Expanding Creative Imagination in Children (Ages 3-80) Through Active Perception.* Institute for the Study and Development of Human Potential, 1981.

Hoard, E. *Getting Kids Ready to Take On the World*. Phoenix, AZ: Kathy Kolbe Concept, Inc., 1983.

Karnes, M.B. *The Underserved: Our Young Gifted Children*. Reston, VA: Council for Exceptional Children, 1920 Association Drive, 22091. 1983.

Mitchell, Patricia B., ed. *An Advocate's Guide to Building Support for Gifted and Talented Education*. National Association of State Boards of Education, 444 N. Capitol St. N.W., Washington, DC, 20001, 1981.

Rimm, Sylvia B. *Underachievement Syndrome: Causes and Cures*. Watertown, WI: Apple Publishing, 1988.

Stein, Morris I. *Gifted, Talented, and Creative Young People*. N.Y.: Garland, 1986.

Sternberg, Robert J. *Beyond IQ*. New York: Cambridge University Press, 1985.

Torrance, E. Paul *Gifted Children in the Classroom*. New York: MacMillan Co., 1965.

Vail, Priscilla L. *Smart Kids with School Problems: Things to Know and Ways to Help*. New York: E. P. Dutton, 1987.

Whitmore, Joanne. *Giftedness, Conflict and Underachievement*. Boston: Allyn and Bacon, 1980.

Appendixes

ASSOCIATIONS DEVOTED TO GIFTED CHILDREN AND THEIR PARENTS

American Association for Gifted
    Children
P.O. Box 2745
Dayton, OH 45401

The Gifted Child Society, Inc.
190 Rock Road
Glen Rock, NJ 07452

National Association for Gifted
    Children
5100 N. Edgewood Drive
St. Paul, MN 55112

The Association for the Gifted
    (TAG)
Council for Exceptional Children
Division for Early Childhood
1920 Association Drive
Reston, VA 22091

Supporting Emotional Needs of the
    Gifted
Wright State University
P.O. Box 1102
Dayton, OH 45401

PUBLICATIONS

G/C/T Publishing Co., Inc.
P.O. Box 6448
Mobile, AL 36660-0448

Gifted Child Monthly
P.O. Box 115
Sewell, NJ 08080

Gifted Child Today (Formerly
    G/C/T)
P.O. Box 66707
Mobile, AL 36660

ICG Journal
Illinois Council for the Gifted
633 Forest Ave.
Wilmette, IL 60091

The New Challenge: Reaching and
    Teaching the Gifted Child
PO Box 299
Carthage, IL 62321-0299

Preschool Perspectives (Column on
    gifted children, by Rita Haynes
    Blocksom)
P.O. Box 7525
Bend, OR 97708

PRISM Magazine, Inc.
1040 Bayview Drive, Suite 223
Ft. Lauderdale, FL 33304

Roeper Review
Roeper City & County School
P.O. Box 329
Bloomfield Hills, MI 48013

Understanding Our Gifted
P.O. Box 3489
Littleton, CO 80122
Edited by Dr. Linda Silverman, this
publication, which premiered in
September 1988, has a special con-
cern with helping parents and
educators recognize and nurture
giftedness in the early years.

Ventura County Superintendent of
    Schools
Attn: LTI Publications
535 East Main Street
Ventura, CA 93009

Zephyr Press Learning Materials
430 S. Essex Lane
Tucson, AZ 85718

PUBLISHERS

Blue Marble
118 N. Ft. Thomas Avenue
Ft. Thomas, KY 41075

DOK (Disseminators of Knowledge)
Box 605
East Aurora, NY 14052

Free Spirit Publishing
4904 Zenith Avenue S.
Minneapolis, MN 55410

Gifted & Talented Publications, Inc.
P.O. Box 115
Sewell, NJ 08080

Montessori Matters and E-Z
    Learning Materials
701 E. Columbia Avenue
Cincinnati, OH 45215

NL Associates, Inc.
Box 1199
Hightstown, NJ 08520

Teachers College Press
Columbia University
1234 Amsterdam Avenue
New York, NY 10027

Trillium Press, Inc.
P.O. Box 921 Madison Sq. Sta.
New York, NY 10159

CHILDREN'S MAGAZINES

Highlights for Children
2300 West Fifth Avenue
P.O. Box 269
Columbus, OH 43272-0002

Your Big Backyard (for
    preschoolers) and Ranger Rick
National Wildlife Federation
141 15th Street N.W.
Washington, DC 20046

Cricket
Open Court Publishing (Literature,
    various styles: poetry, folktales,
    fantasy, fiction and nonfiction)
P.O. Box 2670
Boulder, CO 80322

Cobblestone (focuses on U.S
    history)
Box 939
Farmingdale, NY 11737

National Geographic World
17th and M Streets N.W.
Washington, DC 20036

Creative Kids (Writings and
    artwork by gifted children)
P.O. Box 637
100 Pine Avenue
Holmes, PA 19043

3-2-1 Contact (On science and
   technology)
E=Mc Square
200 Watt Street
P.O. Box 2933
Boulder, CO 80322

Odyssey, c/o Astro Media Corp.
   (Focus on space and astronomy)
6535 E. St. Paul Avenue
P.O. Box 92788
Milwaukee, WI 53202

Sports Illustrated
   for Kids
P.O. Box 830609
Birmingham, AL 35283-0609

GAMES, RESOURCES, PUZZLES, ETC.

Resources for the Gifted, Inc.
P.O. Box 15050
Phoenix, AZ 85060

TOYS

Constructive Playthings
1227 East 199th Street
Grandview, MO 64030

Toys to Grow On
2695 E. Dominguez Street
P.O. Box 17
Long Beach, CA 90801

Childcraft
20 Kilmer Road
P.O. Box 3143
Edison, NJ 08818-3143

Aristoplay, LTD
P.O. Box 7028
Ann Arbor, MI 48107

ADVANCED BEHAVIOR COMPARISONS:

The following table, prepared by Eleanor G. Hall and Nancy Skinner in *Somewhere to Turn: Strategies for Parents of the Gifted and Talented*, merely projects a standard margin of thirty percent earlier than typical behavior. By themselves these numbers don't present empirical evidence of a child's promise. The table is not an end unto itself, but rather a useful quick-reference index to help in early identification. Many but not all gifted children often demonstrate advanced development in these areas.

Developmental Guidlines for IdentifyingGifted-Preschoolers

General Motor Ability	Normal Months	30% More Advanced
Lifts chin up when lying stomach down	1	0.7
Holds up both head and chest	2	1.4
Rolls over	3	2.1
Sits up with support	4	2.8
Sits alone	7	4.9
Stands with help	8	5.6
Stands holding on	9	6.3
Creeps	11	7.7
Stands alone well	11	7.7
Walks alone	12.5	8.75
Walks, creeping is discarded	15	10.5
Creeps up stairs	15	10.5
Walks up stairs	18	12.6
Seats self in chair	18	12.6
Turns pages of book	18	12.6
Walks down stairs one hand held	21	14.7
Walks up stairs holds rail	21	14.7
Runs well, no falling	24	16.8
Walks up and down stairs alone	24	16.8
Walks on tiptoe	30	21.0
Jumps with both feet	30	21.0
Alternates feet when walking up stairs	36	25.2
Jumps from bottom step	36	25.2
Rides tricycle using pedals	36	25.2
Skips on one foot only	48	33.6
Throws ball	48	33.6
Skips alternating feet	60	42.0

(continued on next page)

Fine Motor Ability	Normal Months	30% More Advanced
Grasps handle of spoon but lets go quickly	1	0.7
Vertical eye coordination	1	0.7
Plays with rattle	3	2.1
Manipulates a ball, is interested in detail	6	4.2
Pulls string adaptively	7	4.9
Shows hand preference	8	5.6
Holds object between fingers and thumb	9	6.3
Holds crayon adaptively	11	7.7
Pushes car alone	11	7.7
Scribbles spontaneously	13	9.1
Drawing imitates stroke	15	10.5
Folds paper once imitatively	21	14.7
Drawing imitates V stroke and circular stroke	24	16.8
Imitates V and H strokes	30	21.0
Imitates bridge with blocks	36	25.2
Draws person with two parts	48	33.6
Draws unmistakable person with body	60	42.0
Copies triangle	60	42.0
Draws person with neck, hands, clothes	72	50.4

Cognitive Language	Normal Months	30% More Advanced
Social smile at people	1.5	1.05
Vocalizes four times or more	1.6	1.12
Visually recognizes mother	2	1.4
Searches with eyes for sound	2.2	1.54
Vocalizes two different sounds	2.3	1.61
Vocalizes four different syllables	7	4.9.
Says "da-da" or equivalent	7.9	5.53
Responds to name, no-no	9	6.3
Looks at pictures in book	10	7.0
Jabbers expressively	12	8.4
Imitates words	12.5	8.75
Has speaking vocabulary of three words (other than ma-ma and da-da)	14	9.8
Has vocabulary of 4-6 words including names	15	10.5
Points to one named body part	17	11.9
Names one object (What is this?)	17.8	12.46
Follows direction to put object in chair	17.8	12.46
Has vocabulary of 10 words	18	12.6
Has vocabulary of 20 words	21	14.7
Combines two or three words spontaneously	21	14.7
Jargon is discarded, 3 word sentences	24	16.8
Uses, I, me, you	24	16.8
Names three or more objects on a picture	24	16.8
Is able to identify 5 or more objects	24	16.8
Gives full name	30	21.0
Names 5 objects on a picture	30	21.0
Identifies 7 objects	30	21.0
Is able to tell what various objects are used for	30	21.0
Counts (enumerates) objects to three	36	25.2
Identifies the sexes	36	25.2

Reprinted by permission of the publisher from Eleanor G. Hall and Nancy Skinner in SOME-WHERE TO TURN: STRATEGIES FOR PARENTS OF THE GIFTED AND TALLENTED from the series Perspectives on Gifted and Talented Education, Elizabeth Neuman, ed. New York, Teachers College Press, © 1980 by Teachers College, Columbia Universtiy, pp. 2-4.

STATE OF MISSOURI
PARENTS AS TEACHERS PROGRAM
SKILL- CONCEPT DEVELOPMENT CHECKLISTS

The activities on the following several pages checklists are grouped by areas of development and are sequenced according to difficulty. Matching the lists to the child's developing abilities several times a year will help parents identify the strengths and weaknesses of their child, spotlight any areas that might benefit from intervention, and plan the educational program that will work best for the child. The time- period headings refer to the approximate ranges when behaviors may be noticed, but is not specifically intended to indicate advanced or delayed development, nor identify characteristics of giftedness. Formulated by the Parents as Teachers program in Missouri for their parent-educators; reprinted by permission of the Fergusson-Florissant school district, Florissant, MO.

SKILLS CHECKLIST FOR BIRTH TO 12 MONTHS

Ferguson-Florissant School District
Early Education Program

Cognitive Language

Birth to 3 weeks

Moods shift quickly
Vocalizes at random (other than crying)[*]
Responds to sound of bell[*]
Regards person momentarily

3 weeks to 3 months

Smiles or coos to adult voices
Cries to express discomfort (hunger, cold, wet, etc.)

---

[*]   basic skills

Moves body in response to noises
Smiles at sound of familiar voice[*]
Vocalizes single sounds
Searches with eyes for sound (side to side only)
Anticipates breast or bottle[*]
Alternates glance between 2 visual targets
Follows visually at point where slowly moving object disappeared
Begins babbling[*]

3 months to 6 months

Vocalizes emotional state (anger or pleasure)[*]
Attempts repetition of string of sounds[*]
Directs sounds and gestures toward objects
Localizes sounds heard at ear level
Refuses food when full

6 months to 12 months

Raises arms to be lifted up[*]
Waves bye-bye[*]
Plays peek-a-boo
Understands firm voice; meaning of "no"
Responds consistently to own name[*]
Differentiates family from strangers
Retrieves desired toy
Claps hands upon verbal request
Localizes sounds heard beside and at ear level
Empties containers to obtain objects inside
Understands command words
Searches for partially hidden object[*]

Gross Motor

Birth to 3 weeks

Startle reflex is strong

Kicks legs reciprocally
Waves arms symmetrically
Turns head to either side when lying on stomach[*]
Lifts head and chest to 45-degree angle[*]
Wobbles head when held in upright position
Attempts to roll from side to stomach
Raises head when held in vertical suspension

3 months to 6 months

Grasps feet with hands when lying on back
Lifts chest with arms when lying on stomach[*]
Rolls over from stomach to back
Holds head erect in sitting position
Assists when pulled to sitting
Sits with support
Rocks on abdomen
Curls toes
Bears partial weight on feet while supported[*]

6 months to 9 months

Assists when pulled to sitting with no head lag[*]
Bears most of weight on legs (knees flex)
Pushes up on hands and knees and rocks
Crawls homolaterally (pulling with both arms simultaneously)
Crawls bilaterally (alternating one side of body at a time)
Crawls reciprocally (alternating arm and leg of opposite side)
Rolls from back to stomach[*]
Sits alone for 60 seconds
Extends arms to front and side when toppled from sitting position
Begins to roll into sitting position
Assumes sitting position without assistance
Picks up objects while sitting unattended

9 months to 12 months

Goes from sitting to prone position
Bears full weight on legs*
Pulls to standing using support*
When standing, keeps feet straight
Creeps bilaterally (alternating one side of body at a time; stomach up)*
Creeps reciprocally (alternating arm and leg of opposite sides;
  stomach up)*
Lowers self to floor from standing position*
Walks with hand held (less than 5 steps)
Lifts one foot off floor while standing

Fine Motor

Birth to 3 weeks

Grasping reflex is strong*
Follows moving object (90 degrees) visually

3 weeks to 3 months

Follows moving object (180 degrees) visually past midline*
Looks at hands
Randomly swipes toward dangling object*
Grasps objects placed in both hands
Resists toy pull*
Clenches hands (fists) while awake

3 months to 6 months

Stares prolonged period at object*
Turns head to follow objects visually
Demonstrates scissor (palmar) grasp
Reaches purposefully for objects out of range
Transfers objects hand to mouth - (food)*
Bangs objects on high chair
Clenches hands (not fisted) loosely while awake

6 months to 9 months

> Rolls or flings toys awkwardly
> Uses scooping hand motion to obtain objects (inferior pincer grasp)
> Reaches for toy with one hand[*]
> Recovers fallen toys
> Puts toys in mouth
> Transfers objects hand to hand[*]

9 months to 12 months

> Places rings on spindle
> Picks up small objects with thumb and forefinger (fine
>   pincer grasp)[*]
> Pokes with isolated index finger
> Pulls at peg from pegboard
> Drops cubes willfully[*]
> Manipulates two objects simultaneously rotating wrist

Self-Care

Birth to 3 months

> Demonstrates sucking reflex[*]
> Demonstrates rooting reflex[*]

3 months to 6 months

> Recognizes and reaches for bottle[*]
> Gums and swallows food
> Avoids biting down automatically

6 months to 9 months

> Feeds self small pieces of finger foods[*]
> Holds cracker or cookie

Bites cracker
Chews cracker

9 months to 12 months

Holds own bottle
Holds cup to drink with both hands (needs assistance)[*]
Begins to hold spoon
Licks food from spoon
Remains dry 1 to 2 hours at a time
Remains cooperatively passive while being dressed or undressed
Ceases drooling

ONE-YEAR-OLD SKILLS CHECKLIST

Cognitive Language

12 to 18 months

Identifies own image in mirror[*]
Imitates words[*]
Uses jargon[*]
Says ma-ma and da-da appropriately
Responds to "no-no" (not always consistently)
Visually attends to named family members or pets
Localizes sound above ear level
Points to objects upon request[*]
Names 2 common objects upon request
Responds to own name
Indicates wants[*]
Uses vocabulary of 4 or 5 words
Imitates actions of adults[*]

18 to 24 months

Imitates simple sounds or words on request[*]
Uses simple 2-word sentences

Shows 3 body parts upon request
Sorts 2 different types of objects
Recognizes names of familiar objects, persons, pets
Points to pictures of familiar objects
Uses 6 to 20 words and understands many more*
Refers to self by name
Stacks 3 rings by size*
Points to 6 common objects*

Gross Motor

12 to 18 months

Stands up alone*
Pushes self on riding toy*
Picks up objects from floor while maintaining balance*
Climbs into chair*
Walks well with smooth starts and stops*
Walks upstairs with hand held*
Walks backwards*

18 to 24 months

Throws ball overhanded*
Walks down stairs with hand held*
Runs fairly well*
Pulls wheeled toys
Pushes and pulls large toys

Fine Motor

12 to 18 months

Places one form into a formboard*
Grasps 2 objects in one hand*
Builds tower (2-4 cubes)*
Places large pegs repeatedly in a pegboard*
Dumps small objects from a bottle
Turns pages of cardboard book

18 to 24 months

Imitates strokes with crayon[*]
Stacks 5 rings on spindle
Builds tower (6 cubes)[*]
Dumps objects from bottle spontaneously[*]
Turns pages of picture book
Imitates vertical line (within 30 degrees)[*]
Unscrews lids

Self-Care

12 to 18 months

Begins to use spoon
Drinks from cup using both hands
Chews well
Extends arms or legs cooperatively while dressing

18 to 24 months

Spoon feeds self entire meal (some spills)
Drinks from cup independently, using both hands
Unwraps food before eating
Requests food (word or gesture)
Takes off clothes without fasteners
Imitates self-care activities without actual grooming

TWO-YEAR-OLD SKILLS CHECKLIST

Cognitive Skills

Refers to self by name
Associates use with common objects[*]
Matches two color samples[*]
Points to big and little objects[*]
Develops ability to anticipate consequences ("Fire will burn.")[*]
Points to six body parts when named[*]
Names eight pictured objects[*]
Imitates the actions of adults

Identifies boy and girl
Identifies own gender
Places objects: in   on   under
Names one color
Understands concept of "one" and "two"
Repeats two digits
Indicates age by fingers
Has active interest in television and books
Pretends[*]

Language Skills

Follows a one-stage command (e.g., "Put the block on the table.")[*]
Explains "No" with two words (e.g., "No cookie.")
Verbalizes wants (e.g., "Want water.")[*]
Uses plural words (e.g., socks)
Uses p - b - m sounds
Puts together two or more words to form simple sentences[*]
Describes what happened in two or three words[*]
Can ask a question (e.g., "Where's Daddy?")[*]
Uses pronouns: I   You   Me
Says or sings a nursery rhyme

Self-Help

Helps put things away
Lifts and drinks from cup and replaces on table
Spoon feeds without spilling[*]
Removes coat or dress
Unzips zippers
Can sometimes put on socks
Dries own hands
Puts on coat unassisted
Eliminates when placed on potty chair[*]
Verbalizes toilet needs fairly consistently[*]
Pours from pitcher
Remains dry through night

Social

Shows both dependence and independence on adults[*]
Watches other children play
Shows curiosity and interest in his surroundings
Shows pride in accomplishments
Uses adults as a resource for help
Snatches and grabs toys
Initiates own play activities
Begins interacting somewhat in parallel play

Gross Motor

Throws a small object two feet
Jumps with two feet together
Rolls ball forward
Walks on tiptoes two steps
Catches a rolled ball
Runs forward ten feet[*]
Uses same foot to lead when walking up steps
Walks up stairs alone (both feet on each step)
Walks down stairs alone (both feet on each step)
Jumps a broad jump
Pedals a tricycle

Fine Motor

Grasps cube with fingers
Inserts large peg into pegboard[*]
Stirs liquid with spoon
Strings five large beads
Rolls, pounds and squeezes clay
Draws vertical line (within 30° of sample line)
Copies a circle
Draws horizontal line
Fills and dumps containers with sand
Turns single pages
Works 5- to 6-piece puzzle
Turns door handles
Turns handle of egg beater
Builds 12-block tower

THREE-YEAR-OLD SKILLS CHECKLIST

Language

Receptive Language

1. Understands use of concrete objects
2. Pantomimes use of objects ("Show me what you do with a toothbrush.")
3. Understands opposites:
   - up-down
   - stop-go
   - hot-cold
   - open-closed
   - happy-sad
   - fast-slow
4. Understands prepositions:
   - in
   - over
   - on
   - top
   - in front of
   - out
   - under
   - off
   - bottom
   - in back of
5. Listens to short stories[*]
6. Follows 2 directions[*]
7. Pairs related objects and pictures
8. Classifies pictures by pointing ("Point to all the animals.")
9. Sequences pictured events from a familiar story[*]
10. Demonstrates inductive reasoning skills[*]
11. Demonstrates variety of ways to perform in a given situation

Expressive Language

12. Names pictures of common objects
13. Names body parts:
    - head
    - arms
    - legs
    - feet
    - hands
    - knees
    - chin
    - face parts
14. States function of major body parts:
    - eyes
    - nose
    - hands
    - ears
    - mouth
    - feet
15. Asks simple questions using "who," "what," "where," and "why"
16. Answers "who," "what," and "where" questions[*]
17. Speaks in 6-8 word sentences[*]
18. Uses present progressive verb (Ex: is doing)[*]
19. Uses past tense ("He walked home.")
20. Uses pronouns correctly: ("I" "you" "me" "he" "she")[*]
21. Tells actions in pictures ("The girl is swinging.")
22. Tells use of pictured items
23. Identifies and describes objects by touch
24. Identifies what's missing from a picture

25. Memorizes and repeats a fingerplay or song*
26. Answers a question regarding physical needs
27. Tells own sex and age and full name
28. Names missing object that is removed from a group of three
29. Recalls 3 objects that are visually presented.
30. Repeats simple sentences of 6 words ("I am a great big boy.")
31. Repeats a sequence of 3 numbers
32. Sequences a series of 3 pictures to tell and describe story
33. Responds correctly to "If,_____, What_____?" questions
34. Understands sentences and questions as indicated by relevant response*

Math

Recognizing Colors and Shapes

1. Matches shapes*
   • circle   • square   • triangle   • rectangle
2. Points to appropriate shape upon command*
3. Labels shapes
   • circle   • square   • triangle   • rectangle
4. Recognizes straight and curved lines
5. Matches colors*
   • red   • yellow   • blue   • brown
   orange   • green   • black*
6. Points to appropriate color upon request*
   • blue   • yellow   • green   • red
   • orange   • brown   • black   • purple
7. Names the three basic colors

Counting

8. Rote counts from 1 to 5*
9. Counts out objects up to 5*
10. Understands number concepts   • 1   • 2   • 3   • other?

Size Differences: Quantitative Concepts

11. Arranges 3 objects by size (small, middle, large)
12. Understands concepts of full and empty
13. Points to which of two sticks is longer
14. Understands   • big   • little*

15. Distinguishes between concepts of "some" and "all."

Classifying

16. Sorts objects into two given categories
(size, shape, color, etc.)*
17. Constructs sets of up to 5 blocks when given a model*

Patterning

18. Reproduces a pattern of three objects when visually displayed*

Gross Motor

1. Drops and catches a ball once
2. Catches a large ball (from 5 to 8 foot distance):*
   • with arms and elbows at side of body
   • with arms slightly extended from body
3. Throws a ball overhand*
4. Throws a bean bag

Body Coordination and Balance

5. Walks • up stairs   • down stairs
   alternating feet, one step per tread, at least 4 steps
6. Walks forward and backward on an 8-foot line*
7. Jumps with both feet
8. Jumps over 6- to 7-inch barrier with both feet
9. Stands on one foot without losing balance*
10. Hops on one foot 2 or more times
11. Kicks a ball with one foot
12. Walks on tiptoe
13. Imitates actions*

Fine Motor

1. Closes fist and wiggles thumb
2. Works with playdough*
3. Pastes with index finger
4. Builds tower*
5. Imitates building "bridge" with cubes

6. Strings at least 4 one-half inch beads
7. Screws and unscrews nuts, bolts and lids
8. Hammers
9. Puts together a 3- to 7-piece puzzle[*]
10. Pours rice or sand
11. Holds crayon with fingers rather than fist
12. Paints with a large brush on large piece of paper (18" x 24")
13. Begins to draw human figure (usually head and legs)[*]
14. Copies[*]
    - horizontal line   • circle   • diagonal line
    - vertical line   • cross
15. Draws between two straight lines
16. Uses kitchen tongs
17. Uses scissors, but does not necessarily follow lines
18. Copies letters: H, T, L

Personal Objectives

(List)

FOUR-YEAR-OLD SKILLS CHECKLIST

Language

Receptive Language

1. Listens to directions for games and activities[*]
2. Follows directions sequentially[*] • 2-step   • 3-step
3. Listens to stories
4. Demonstrates position orientation concepts:

• top	• over	• around	• first[**]
• bottom	• under	• through	• last[**]
• in	• in front of	• between	• middle[**]
• out	• in back of	• beside	• before[**]
• next to	• after[**]		

5. Pantomimes use of objects such as toothbrush, cup, spoon
6. Acts out a familiar story or nursery rhyme as teacher recites
7. Recognizes which does not belong in a group of 4 items

[**] extending skills

8. Sequences pictures to tell a story or describe a cooking experience
   •3   •4   •5 pictures*
9. Chooses pairs of objects that rhyme (boat-goat, chain-plane)
10. Distinguishes words that begin with the same sound (book-boy)**
11. Associates a letter with its sound in spoken words**
12. Demonstrates understanding of position orientation concepts on
    a flat surface (e.g., paper)**
13. Proposes alternate ways of:**
    •using an object   •art experiences
    •movement activities   •story endings

Expressive Language

14. Speaks in sentences of 8, 10 or more words*
15. Touches and names parts of the body:

•head	•eyes	•hands	•arms
•feet	•legs	•nose	•mouth
•ears	•neck	•trunk	•ankle
•knee**	•shoulder**	•wrist**	•elbow**
•heel**			

16. Tells functions of body parts:

•	•head	•eyes	•hands	•arms
•feet		•legs	•nose	•mouth
•ears		•neck	•trunk	•ankle
•knee**		•shoulder**	•wrist**	•elbow**
•heel**				

17. Verbalizes songs or fingerplays*
18. Makes relevant verbal contributions in small group discussion*
19. Verbalizes opposite analogies or relationships*
    (Brother is a boy; sister is a____ .)
20. Tells definition of common objects
21. Identifies and uses words opposite in meaning using visual or
    tactual clues (up-down—hot-cold).
22. Describes objects using the following attributes:
    •color   •shape
    •size   •use   •composition
23. Uses more than one attribute when describing a single object
24. Describes a picture with three statements*
25. Verbalizes: full name, age,** address,** birthday,** phone number
26. Describes objects by touch as:
    •rough-smooth   •thick-thin   •hard-soft

27. Retells short story of 5 sentences in sequence using own words
28. Demonstrates understanding of new ideas and vocabulary
29. Identifies verbally the letters in first name
30. Identifies verbally the letters in last name
31. Identifies many letters of the alphabet:
    • upper case   • lower case
32. Sequences letters in: • first name   • last name
33. Dictates own experience stories
34. Describes observations made of changes in food during cooking
    activities (e.g., color, texture, form)
35. Makes a simple comparison in terms of different or same[*]
36. Predicts what will happen next in a story or situation
37. Predicts realistic outcomes of events
38. Responds to questions such as: What if?   How many ways?
39. Responds correctly to "How" questions (How do you take a bath?)
40. Names two words that rhyme (in a group of 3)[*]
41. Supplies rhyming word to rhyme with a word given by teacher[**]
42. Interprets the main idea of:[**] • a picture   • a story
43. Makes inferences from a story[**]
44. Distinguishes between fact and fantasy[**]
45. Relates cause to effect (If you never eat, then what will happen?)[**]

Math

Colors and Shapes

1. Points to colors
    • yellow   • purple   • black
    • orange   • green   • white
    • red   • blue   • brown
2. Names colors:[*]
    • yellow   • purple   • black
    • orange   • green   • white
    • red   • blue   • brown
3. Points to shapes:
    • triangle   • circle   • square
    • rectangle   • diamond[**]

4. Names shapes:*
- triangle
- circle
- square
- rectangle
- diamond**

Counting

5. Counts from 1 to [what?]*
6. Understands ordinal positions:** :
   - first
   - second
   - last
   - middle

Size

7. Identifies size differences:
   - long
   - large
   - thick**
   - short
   - small
   - thin**
8. Understands terms •bigger than •smaller than
9. Orders size differences:
   - big, bigger, biggest
   - small, smaller, smallest
   - short, shorter, shortest
   - long, longer, longest
10. Sequences objects from shortest to longest (7 objects)*

Quantitative Concepts

11. Compares objects as to weight ("Which is heavier? lighter?")
12. Understands concepts of:
    - full
    - half-full
    - empty
13. Graphing - comparing objects to:* •more •less
14. Understands the concepts of:
    - more than
    - most**
    - less than
    - least**
15. Measures and compares:
    - length of object
    - width of object
    - volume
16. Understands fractions:
    - 1/2
    - 1/4**
    - whole

Classifying

17. Classifies objects using one attribute:*
    - color
    - size
    - shape
    - texture

18. Classifies objects using:
   - •2 attributes ("Put the little squares here.")
   - •3 attributes ("Put the big red circles here.")**
19. Determines how to classify objects by:**
   - •color ("I put all the blue together.")
   - •size ("I put all the big ones here.")
   - •shape ("I put all the circles here.")

Patterning

20. Copies pattern by color, shape or size*
21. Extends a pattern by color, shape or size
22. Creates own pattern

Sets and Numerals

Sets
23. Identifies a set as a collection of objects having a common property (e.g., size, color, shape, function, etc.)
24. Establishes a one-to-one correspondence, counting each object once:*
   - •3 objects   •5 objects   • objects
25. Constructs equal set to sample set
26. Distinguishes between equivalent and non-equivalent sets through comparing
27. Understands number concepts: •3 •4 •5
28. Identifies and constructs sets containing number of objects:*
   - •0 to 5   •6 to 10
29. Identifies an empty set as having no members
30. Identifies "0" as a symbol for an empty set
31. Constructs set with (one more) than sample set
32. Understands that each number is one more than the preceding number. ("What is one more than 2?")
33. Forms a new set by joining two sets
34. Understands subsets of a number

Numerals
35. Recognizes cardinal numerals
36. Associates cardinal numerals with corresponding sets*

37. Orders the cardinal numerals in sequence
38. Solves simple verbal problems using numerals.** ("If you have two pieces of candy and I give you one more, how many will you have?")
39. Identifies penny, nickel, dime and quarter**

Science

40. Predicts outcome of experiment, using concrete objects. (What will float? What will sink?)
41. Observes changes in the seasons
42. Discovers how things change

Personal Objectives

(List)

Gross Motor

Arm-Eye Coordination

1. Catches a ball away from body with hands only*
2. Bounces and catches a ball four consecutive times with both hands
3. Throws a ball with direction*
4. Throws balls in the air and catches by self
5. Catches a bean bag in a scoop
6. Hits an 18" to 24" flat target at a distance of 6 feet with a ball or bean bag (4 out of 5 times)

Balance

7. Walks a line 8 feet long
8. Walks a balance beam 8 feet long*
9. Stops and picks up bean bag in middle of balance beam
10. Steps over object on balance beam
11. Walks backward on an 8 ft. balance beam without stepping off
12. Walks forward, eyes looking at target; must not look down

13. Produces following motions:*
- •hops on right foot - 4 times
- •balances on right foot
- •balances on left foot
- •hops on left foot - 4 times
- •5 sec. •10 sec.
- •5 sec. •10 sec.

14. Jumps 6-inch-high obstacle, landing on both feet
15. Kicks 10-inch ball to large target 10 feet away
16. Stops movement activity on signal

General Movement

17. Claps or marches in time with music*
18. Responds to rhythms with appropriate body movements
19. Walks alone down stairs
20. Child is able to reproduce following motions:
- •walks backward
- •runs
- •marches
- •gallops
- •runs on tiptoes
- •skips

Fine Motor

Hand-Eye Coordination

1. Follows a sequence of holes when lacing
2. Works a puzzle of 8 or more pieces*
3. Uses crayon or pencil to express his own ideas
4. Follows dot-to-dot series to form an object; numerals 1 to 10
5. Manipulates pencil or crayon to complete a maze
6. Includes major body parts and features in drawing a person*
7. Adds details to body drawing
8. Reproduces shapes:*
- •with model
- •circle
- •triangle
- •without model
- • square
- •rectangle
- •circle •square
- •triangle •rectangle

9. Prints name: •with model •without model
10. Reproduces numerals: •with model •without model
11. Controls brush and paint
12. Uses scissors with control: •straight line •curved line

Finger Strength and Dexterity

13. Manipulates clay into forms and objects
14. Pastes using one finger
15. Touches thumb to all fingers on same hand
16. Folds and creases paper
17. Uses right or left hand consistently

Eye Tracking

18. Works from top to bottom in visual-motor activities when directed
19. Follows left-to-right progression in tracking and drawing most of
       the time[*]

Personal-Social

1. Expresses feelings in words
2. Works and plays cooperatively with other children
3. Participates with others in large groups
4. Takes turns and shares
5. Shows concerns for others and their property
6. Takes initiative in learning
7. Pays attention and concentrates on a task
8. Consistently completes a task
9. Works cooperatively with adults
10. Feels good about himself/herself
11. Is courteous to others
12. Resolves peer conflicts with language or by social means
13. Can separate from parent and engage in activity
14. Reunites well with parents

KINDERGARTEN—BEGINNING PRIMARY SKILLS CHECKLIST

Language

Listening

1. Imitates a rhythmic pattern by clapping.
2. Repeats a series of digits, words or sounds: series of •4 •6
3. Repeats a sentence of at least: •5 words •8 words •10 words
4. Listens to stories for: •15 minutes •30 minutes
5. Follows directions: •2-step •3-step •4-step
6. Listens to story with headphones: •5 min. •10 min. •15 min.

Speaking

1. Labels objects.
2. Expresses personal needs.
3. Speaks in sentences of: •8 words •10 words or more
4. Contributes to group discussion.
5. Expresses feelings verbally.
6. Repeats a poem or fingerplay. •8-line •16-line
7. Tells what is happening in pictures.
8. Demonstrates understanding of relative time concepts.
9. Understands position orientation concepts.
10. Tells identifying personal information:
    •birthday •phone number •address •city
    •state •zip code •last name of family
11. Knows days of the week and months of the year:

	by rote	out of sequence
•days of the week	_____	_____
•months of the year	_____	_____

12. Tells what will happen next in a sequence of pictures.
13. Retells a story: •one read to him •one he has read
14. Dictates own story.
15. Uses complex and compound sentences.
16. Describes objects or story characters.
17. Describes events of past and future experiences.

Reasoning and Thinking Skills

1. Solves simple problem situations.
2. Associates objects.
3. Associates objects according to function.
4. Completes a statement of relationship ("Grass is green; sugar is ————.")
5. Compares in terms of likenesses and differences.
6. Categorizes objects according to three attributes.
7. Sequences pictures to make a story.
8. Summarizes main idea from oral presentation.
9. Uses information to draw simple conclusions.
10. Interprets cause and effect relationships.
11. Infers details from a story or situation.
12. Distinguishes between reality and fantasy.
13. Responds to questions: "What if_____" or "How many ways _____?"

Reading

1. Associates letters and sounds.
2. Associates printed words with objects.
3. Reads own story.
4. Uses pictures for context clues in reading.
5. Reads and comprehends at:
   - •Pre-primer •First Reader
   - •Primer •Second Reader

Phonetic Analysis
1. Tells when 2 words pronounced by teacher do or do not rhyme.
2. Names words that rhyme.
3. Supplies rhyming words to rhyme with a word given by teacher.
4. Distinguishes words that begin with the same sound.
5. Identifies the letter that makes the initial sound.
6. Discriminates ending sounds in words.
7. Identifies the letter that makes the ending sounds.
8. Identifies words that begin with the same consonant blend and the letters that make up the sounds.
9. Recognizes the variant sounds of s, c, and g.
10. Identifies simple two-consonant combinations: ch, sh, th.
11. Identifies the medial sound.

12. Identifies the vowel letter.
13. Recognizes the effect of r, al, and aw on vowel sounds in words.
14. Recognizes and says words in which there is an oi, oy, ou, ow, or ew combination. (Ex: house, boy, soil, cow, new)
15. Identifies the appropriate "oo" combination in words.

Structural Analysis
1. Names upper case letters.
2. Names lower case letters.
3. Selects a rhyming word based on structure.
4. Identifies compound words and specifies the elements of a compound word.
5. Identifies simple contractions and uses them correctly in sentences.
6. Understands root words.
7. Recognizes and understands the use of comparative terms.
8. Determines whether a singular or plural noun should be used.
9. Uses appropriate singular or plural forms of irregular verbs.
10. Identifies the possessive forms of nouns and pronouns in context.
11. Demonstrates his understanding of how root words are modified by prefixes or suffixes.
12. Demonstrates understanding of the use of inflectional endings.
13. Understands abbreviations and symbols.
14. Understands difference between action words and nouns.

Reading Comprehension
1. Senses mood conveyed by the author.
2. Matches pictures with sentences.
3. Follows simple printed directions.
4. Recalls beginning, middle and end of a story.
5. Predicts the outcome of a selection.
6. Identifies words with opposite meanings.
7. Identifies words with similar meanings.
8. Supplies words which correctly complete sentence.
9. Interprets cause-effect relationships.
10. Finds parts of sentences to answer recall questions.
11. Uses context to determine the meaning of a word.
12. Senses implied feelings and/or reactions of story characters.
13. Identifies the main idea of a selection.
14. Recalls facts.
15. Uses homonyms correctly in the context of a sentence.

Creative Expression and Writing
(A)
1. Acts out a familiar story or nursery rhyme as teacher narrates.
2. Reads orally with expression.
3. Participates in choral reading or dramatic reading.
   (B)
1. Writes first and last name.
2. Writes a simple sentence.
3. Expands sentences.
4. Uses capital letters in sentences.
5. Uses correct punctuation at the end of a sentence.
6. Can proofread a simple sentence.
7. Writes a simple sentence that is dictated.
8. Creates a story based on a described or pictured situation.
9. Can write a simple letter.
10. Reads a story and writes a simple book report.

Library and Study Skills

1. Identifies title and author of book.
2. Uses a table of contents.
3. Alphabetizes by first letter, second letter and third letter.
4. Locates words in dictionary.
5. Distinguishes between fiction and nonfiction.

Fine Motor

1. Follows top-to-bottom progression.
2. Follows left-to-right progression.
3. Folds paper into: •halves and quarters •diagonals
4. Uses crayon or pencil with control within a defined area.
5. Controls brush and paint.
6. Uses scissors with control (cuts on line): •straight •curved
7. Connects a dotted outline to make a shape.
8. Pastes using one finger.
9. Holds a pencil correctly.
10. Works a previously unseen puzzle of 10 or more pieces.
11. Includes major body parts and features in drawing a person.
12. Traces objects.
12a. Copies a pattern from board to paper.
13. Writes basic strokes.

14. Writes upper and lower case letters correctly.
15. Reproduces numerals.
16. Uses lined paper correctly.

Math

Math

1. Identifies size differences:
   - big
   - long
   - large
   - wide
   - thick
   - little
   - short
   - small
   - narrow
   - thin
2. Orders size differences:
   - big, bigger, biggest
   - small, smaller, smallest
   - short, shorter, shortest
   - long, longer, longest
3. Distinguishes between concepts of "some" and "all."
4. Predicts which object is heavier or lighter.
5. Estimates and compares lengths (equal, shorter, shortest, longer, longest).
6. Uses a bar graph to compare results.
7. Uses the thermometer to measure heat or cold.
8. Measures a liter.
9. Identifies coins:
   - penny
   - nickel
   - dime
   - quarter
   - half-dollar
   - dollar
10. Counts value of pennies and nickels and dimes (totaling 99¢ or less).
11. Forms a given collection of monies to a given value up to 99¢.
12. Measures lengths in: •centimeters •inches

Time Concepts

1. Associates events with:
   - day
   - night
   - morning
   - afternoon
   - evening
2. Observes the seasonal changes and their weather.
3. Identifies date and day of the week.
4. Maintains a calendar for a month.
5. Identifies concept of: •tomorrow •yesterday •today
6. Tells time to: •hour •half-hour •minutes past hour
7. Names months of the year.

Place Value and Counting

1. Identifies a set as a collection of objects having a common property (size, color, shape, function, etc.)
2. Identifies and constructs sets containing 0-5 objects.
3. Understands one-to-one correspondence.
4. Constructs equal set to sample set.
5. Counts sets of objects 11-19.
6. Identifies given set of objects in varying formations.
7. Constructs set with one more member than a sample set.
8. Identifies objects in a sequence using first, last, next, middle.
9. Understands concepts:
   - more than
   - greater than
   - most
   - less than
   - fewer than
   - fewest
10. Counts from one through   •100 •1000
11. Understands:
    - first
    - second
    - third
    - fourth
    - fifth
12. Determines which of two numbers (10 or less) is greater. Writes number sentences using symbols > and <.
13. Understands concept of "one more."
14. Understands that each numeral is one less than the following numeral.
15. Recognizes numerals 1-10.
16. Places cardinal numerals in sequence from 0-10.
17. Writes numerals 1 through: •10 •50 •100
18. Recognizes numerals 10 to 100.
19. Counts by: •10's •5's •2's
20. Tells which of two numerals is greater (100 or less).
21. Counts and names tens and ones.
22. Writes numerals for collection of tens and ones.
23. Writes numerals for multiples of 10 and multiples of 100.

Additions and Sets

1. Associates numeral "0" with an empty set.
2. Associates cardinal numerals with corresponding sets:
   - 0-5
   - 6-10
3. Separates objects into two subsets.
4. Forms a new set by joining two sets.
5. Combines sets to sums of 5.

6. Combines sets to sums of 6-10.
7. Constructs number sentence horizontally and vertically.
8. Recalls from memory the basic addition facts: •0- 5 •6-10
9. Adds sums 11-19.
10. Adds three addends.
11. Adds 2-digit numbers when no regrouping is required.
12. Adds 2-digit numbers when regrouping is required.
13. Completes number sentences when one addend is missing.
14. Adds 3-digit numbers when no regrouping is required.
15. Uses zero in addition and subtraction.

Subtraction

1. Subtracts by taking a subset from the set of objects.
2. Constructs number sentence vertically and horizontally.
3. Recalls from memory the basic subtraction facts: •0- 5 •6-10
4. Subtracts when the greater number is 11-19 and no regrouping
    is required.
5. Subtracts 2-digit numbers when no regrouping is required.
6. Subtracts 2-digit numbers when regrouping is required.
7. Removes a subset from a set to find the remaining subset.

Fractions

1. Identifies concepts of:
    •one-half   •one-fourth   •one-third   •whole
2. Correctly divides whole into fractional parts.

Geometry

1. Correctly identifies:
    •triangle   •circle   •square   •rectangle
    •diamond
2. Names:
    •triangle   •circle   •square   •rectangle
    •diamond   •ovals
3. Traces shapes:
    with model   *without model*
    •circle   •square   •circle   •square
    •triangle   •rectangle   •triangle   •rectangle
    •diamond   •oval   •diamond   •oval

4. Completes a pattern in alternating color, shape and/or size.
5. Reproduces a simple pattern of shapes from memory:
   •3 items   •4 items   •5 items
6. Identifies shapes of solid objects: cone, pyramid, cylinder, sphere, cube, rectangular solid.

Problem Solving

1. Classifies objects by:
   •color   •size   •shape   •texture
2. Determines how to classify objects by:
   •color   •size   •shape
3. Solves word problems by using concrete objects.
4. Solves problems through logic; using clues, can infer property or identify object that the leader has chosen.
5. Solves word problems by adding or subtracting 2-digit numbers where no regrouping is required.
6. Solves problems that involve addition of quantities of money.
7. Solves problems that involve subtraction of quantities of money.
8. Multiplies two sets (of the same number).

Index